BRUNEL'S HIDDEN KINGDOM

By Geoffrey Tudor

Compiled by Helen Hillard

First Published in Great Britain in 2007 by
Creative Media Publishing

Copyright © Geoffrey Tudor and Helen Hillard 2007

ISBN 0-9546071-2-0

Design and production
Creative Media Ltd, 35 Woodland Park, Paignton, TQ3 2ST
www.mhcreativemedia.co.uk
Layout designed by Nick Wilton

CONTENTS

Brunel's Hidden Kingdom '... the full story of the estate he created and house he planned at Watcombe, Torquay'

Preface   **5**

Foreword   **8**

Introduction   **10**

Chapter 1:   **Launching the Watcombe Adventure:** why the country   **13**
house? – why near Torquay? – Brunel builds up his team

Chapter 2:   **Landowning has its Problems:** trouble over the parish roads –   **27**
more land, and more problems – the need for a
West Country base

Chapter 3:   **Planning the Enterprise:** a water-supply for Watcombe –   **43**
shelter-belts, and the concept of the Great Eastern – Brunel's
Watcombe Garden Book

Chapter 4:   **The Brunel/Forsyth Partnership:** trees, and still more trees –   **58**
'...great knowledge of tree cultivation...'

Chapter 5:   **Brunel's Local Involvements:** the good employer –   **72**
environmental champion – social complexities – Brunels at
the poultry-show

Chapter 6:   **'My Unfortunate Friend, Mr. Watson':** Watson's building   **82**
schemes falter – Brunel to the rescue – Watson's sorry fate

Chapter 7:   **1858: Watcombe Planning still moving forward:** 'I will   **87**
build a house...' – '...the happiest hours of his life...' – 'the
improvement of this property was his chief delight.'

Chapter 8: **The End of the Watcombe Adventure:** at work in the gardens,   **109**
Easter 1858 – Brunel's illness and death – '...admitting any
person to view the grounds.'

Chapter 9: **The Brunel Family and Torquay:** Henry Brunel's   **119**
'Great Bridge at Watcombe' – Watcombe's emotional grip –
purchasers for Watcombe Park

Chapter 10: **The Grounds Mature:** a walk around the park in 1882 –   **124**
a longer walk around the park in 1887

Chapter 11: **Brunel's Heritage at Watcombe:** 'The glory has departed' –   **131**
the Watcombe estate dismantled – the case for preserving
Brunel's landscaping masterpiece

Brunel's Arboretum   **144**

Brunel's Watcombe Estate - The Continuing Story   **151**

Afterword   **152**

Bibliography   **153**

Acknowledgements   **155**

Index   **156**

PREFACE
By Helen and Rick Hillard
Brunel Manor

This book heralds the unlocking of South Devon's greatest secret. Until now, little has been known about the twelve years Isambard Kingdom Brunel was creating his Watcombe estate and planning his magnificent house. This was to have been the fulfilment of his lifelong dream. When he was a young man of twenty one, he wrote of his 'chateaux d'Espagne' or 'castles in the air' as he called them. He set out a number of aspirations that showed he clearly had his eyes firmly fixed on paving his way to fame and fortune through his innovative engineering projects. The list included his desire to build a fine house to reflect the wealth he would achieve. Although his Watcombe venture involved Brunel personally in more time and money than any of his engineering exploits, very little has been written about it until now. Not only does this book unfold the untold story of Brunel the master landscaper and garden designer, but it reflects different endearing aspects of his character. Woven into its pages we see a Brunel in tune with nature, treasuring times at Watcombe with his family, being generous to his estate workers and getting very involved in the local community in a variety of ways.

Henry Brunel's pencil box in which he kept the letter, written to his brother by his father, Isambard Kingdom Brunel, impressing on him the importance of prayer. Image - private collection.

Isambard Kingdom Brunel's Great-great-grandchildren, Lady Vanessa Thomas and Lord Miles Gladwyn at the official opening of the Brunel Manor grounds on Brunel's 200th Birthday Celebrations, 9th April 2006. They are pictured here on the terrace with its stunning view over Torbay in the background. Isambard (Brunel's first son) described this view as "one of the loveliest in that part of Devonshire". © Herald Express, Torquay.

In the 1950s, the house at Watcombe became known as Brunel Manor. It has been owned by The Woodlands House of Prayer Trust since 1963 and is run as a Christian Holiday and Conference Centre. It was suggested that Brunel Manor should participate in the 2006 Brunel 200 Celebrations, a project funded by HLF, involving many Brunel sites throughout the region. What began with the idea of opening up the grounds to visitors a few times during the year was to become the start of a huge project of garden restoration. A former head gardener at Brunel Manor, Andy Maltas, who had returned to work there in 2005, knew that many of Brunel's original features lay hidden under decades of overgrowth. As research was undertaken,

we discovered that Brunel himself had drawn many plans in his sketch books and made very detailed planting notes in his Watcombe Garden Book. He had even measured his growing trees over several years. Using these and other resources, work on restoration began. The funding facilitated the formation of a garden trail with interpretation panels, the production of a detailed map and the setting up of an exhibition showing the history of Brunel at Watcombe. Tree plaques to Brunel's design were commissioned and yew trees in tubs set out on the terrace, as described in his Watcombe Garden Book.

A delightful discovery that came to light during the research was that Brunel had been a man of prayer. A pencil box bearing the initials of his son Henry Brunel was inherited by his great granddaughter. She found that one of the envelopes locked inside it contained a letter that Brunel had written to his son Isambard at the time of the difficult launching of the Great Eastern. This letter, left to his brother Henry as "my most treasured possession", concludes:

"Finally, let me impress upon you the advantage of prayer. I am not prepared to say that the prayers of individuals can be separately and individually granted, that would seem incompatible with the regular movements of the mechanism of the Universe, and it would seem impossible to explain why prayer should be now granted, now refused; but this I can assure you, that I have ever, in my difficulties, prayed fervently, and that – in the end – my prayers have been, or have appeared to me to be, granted, and I have received great comfort."

It seems that Brunel found his property at Watcombe to be a sanctuary away from the pressures of his heavy workload.

He also wanted others to enjoy it and instructed his gardener *'to have the liberty of admitting any person to view the grounds'*. The Woodlands House Of Prayer Trust was established to provide a home where people could receive spiritual and physical rest. It is therefore in keeping with this ethos that the Brunel Manor grounds should be open for others to see and to find rest and refreshment in body, mind and spirit. Brunel's great great granddaughter, Lady Thomas, officially opened the grounds on Brunel's 200th Birthday, April 9th 2006.

The Brunel 200 Celebrations have made this whole venture possible and paved the way for the production of this book. Geoff Tudor's careful and thorough research on this subject has been an inspiration and valuable resource throughout the project and it has been his own dream to see this book become a reality.

Helen and Rick Hillard

FOREWORD

By Angus Buchanan: Author of 'Brunel', 2002

When I.K. Brunel began to think about acquiring a country estate in the 1840s, his mind does not appear to have turned to the Home Counties, close to his Westminster house at the centre of British government and society, nor to the environs of Bristol, where he had established so many creative business relationships.

It ranged instead along the course of the railways he had built or was still in the course of building beyond Bristol to Exeter and on into Devon and Cornwall. He had found convenient bases for family holidays at Weston-super-Mare and Clevedon, on the Somerset coast, and then at Torquay, when he had become engaged on the South Devon Railway. It was here, in the rolling countryside north of the town, that he discovered a site with a panoramic southern vision, close to the coast and easily accessible from his railway. Here he made his first land purchase in 1847, from which would develop the Watcombe Park estate. Once he had established this foothold, Brunel applied himself with characteristic zest to consolidating it through additional purchases, to modifying the road access, and to landscaping the prospect. He also worked out elaborate plans for the house that he proposed to build on the estate, and designed the extensive garden with careful consideration to appropriate tree planting, pathways and water features. The house designed by Brunel was never built, as he died before the foundations could be completed and his family then felt obliged to sell the estate. But he had made considerable progress with the garden by the time of his death, so that terraces had been established, many fine trees had been planted, and a network of well-constructed pathways had been installed.

The present 'Brunel Manor' was subsequently built on the site prepared by Brunel, and until the end of the century the estate was well maintained by the Wrights of Nottingham – a banking family. The estate was then dismembered, and Brunel's designed landscape became obscured by encroaching woodland and by the new suburban houses that were built up to the borders of the old estate. It was from one such modern house that Geoffrey Tudor had the serendipitous experience of discovering Brunel's forgotten creation quite literally at the bottom of his own garden. By crossing the boundary into the enchanted but overgrown woodland beyond, he found sinuous well-made paths surviving amidst the vegetation, with many large but unusual trees emerging from the undergrowth. He gradually explored this magical estate and, by some diligent research in the local and national archives, he found that this was indeed Brunel's garden, and that, contrary to the received opinion amongst scholars of Brunel studies, an amazing part of it was recognisable and capable of restoration.

To the great credit of Geoff Tudor and the present owners of the estate this work of restoration has been undertaken, so that the Brunel Garden has at last become accessible to visitors. Without Geoff's persistence in bringing the existence of this outstanding heritage feature to public notice, and his painstaking research in chasing up the surviving documentary accounts of the estate, it is difficult to believe that this could have been achieved. Nobody is better equipped to describe and explain this unusual but truly astonishing monument to the great engineer, the second centenary of whose birth was celebrated nationally and internationally in 2006. This book is thus most welcome, bringing together the fruit of Geoff Tudor's research over many years and presenting it in a form that is colourful and attractive. It will serve as an excellent Guide to the Brunel Garden, but it is of course more than that, as it is a unique contribution to Brunel studies and a valuable work of scholarship.

Angus Buchanan
University of Bath
February 2007

The Italian Garden before the restoration commenced in 2006   Image: Tracey Elliot-Reep

INTRODUCTION

Brunel was not a man for half-measures. It was on Christmas Eve, 1847, that he sought – in great haste – a reference for a gardener, Alexander Forsyth. He was 'wanted to superintend the formation of a Park, where all is to be done.' Brunel was not prepared to purchase some other man's achievement: Watcombe was to be his own creation. On 6th September 1859, just nine days before he died, Brunel gave orders for the estate to be sold. In two senses Watcombe is 'Brunel's Hidden Kingdom'. Firstly, no detailed account of Brunel's estate building has been written – Rolt dismissed it in a single page as a dream that vanished. Secondly, much of Brunel's landscaping has been covered over or despoiled by neglect, almost as with the Lost Gardens of Heligan – that famous Cornish example of garden rescue.

Brunel's 'Watcombe Adventure' lasted eleven and a half years – more than a third of Brunel's adult life. He began at a time when there was a major slump in railway construction and the Atmospheric System in Devon was nearing disaster. While Watcombe Park was being planted Brunel was:

- Bridging the Tamar and extending his railway to Penzance over magnificent timber viaducts

- Assisting with the Great Exhibition of 1851 and designing the great water towers for the Crystal Palace at Sydenham

- Designing a prefabricated hospital for use in the Crimean War

- Envisaging, designing and launching the *Great Eastern*

- Involved with dock and railway construction in Britain and overseas

Watcombe Park absorbed more personal involvement in time and money than any of Brunel's other ventures. It also demonstrated a genius in landscaping that was recognised by a writer in *The Gardener's Chronicle* in 1887, forty years after the Adventure had begun. In the evening sunshine the contrasting textures and hues on the opposite slope were a wonder to behold, '...a good illustration of what may be done in that direction when the planter knows what he is about.' Brunel knew what he was about – and so, incidentally, did Mary Brunel. Probably their happiest times together were spent at Watcombe, laying out the gardens, planning next year's planting, and recording the growth of trees. Through good fortune Brunel's Garden Notebook – mislaid for many years – has been rediscovered and is now safely housed with other Brunel material at

Bristol University. This book – all in Brunel's scrawling and not easily legible hand – proves beyond doubt that the design of Watcombe Park was as much a product of his genius as any of his bridges, buildings or ships.

True, Watcombe was never completed, and has been sadly neglected and despoiled. Yet it remains the most personal of all memorials of Brunel – more personal than stations and statues and stained glass windows. His *Great Britain* was recovered from the Falkland Islands and brought home to Bristol to be restored: it should surely be possible to salvage Watcombe Park for posterity.

Above: Brunel's Watcombe Garden Book, a simple foolscap notebook, in which he wrote details for water requirements, engine requirements and instructions for tree planting schemes for his Watcombe estate. It also includes drawings of his growing trees, tables recording several years of tree measurements and designs for topiary. The entries date from 1849 - 1858. © University of Bristol

1847	1847
Atmospheric Railway service opens from Exeter to Teignmouth & operates for only one year.	Brunel buys first plot of land at Watcombe and writes on Christmas Eve about engaging Alexander Forsyth as his gardener.

1848	1848
Torre Railway Station opened in Torquay.	Road closures are negotiated in order to create the estate. 50 local men employed to prepare grounds.

1849	1849
Work begins on Chepstow Bridge. Windsor Bridge opened.	Watcombe Lodge is rented as a West Country base for the Brunel family. Brunel's first records of trees in his arboretum.

1850	1850
Appointed to building committee for the Great Exhibition.	Simpsons of Pimlico engaged to install water supply.

1851	1851
Brunel involved with the Great Exhibition, including being chair for the jury for Civil Engineering, Architecture & Building Contrivances. He also assisted in dispensation of the prizes.	Brunel sends his Watcombe estate workers on an all expenses paid holiday to London to visit the Great Exhibition. He buys land at Barn Close to build workers houses and a school/chapel. William Burn draws a plan of the mansion at Watcombe.

1852	1852
Work begins on Paddington Station.	Brunel plants his shelter belts of beech trees.

1853	1853
Work begins on: The Great Eastern, the Royal Albert Bridge and water towers for the Sydenham Crystal Palace.	Watcombe Garden Book started. Sketches and measurements of some of his trees. The Brunels host lavish party for their estate workers and 70 children from Mary Brunel's school at Barton. Wall built between Steps Lane and the turnpike.

1854	1854
Paddington Station completed.	7 wells dug to supply water to the house and grounds. Planting of many trees along the sea walk.

1855	1855
The first type of prefabricated hospital is designed by Brunel to be shipped out to the Renkioi for use during the Crimean War.	Brunel enquires about Prudham stone for his house.

	1856
	George Martin, quantity surveyor, paid for work "...in connection with proposed house at Watcombe."

1857	1857
Balmoral Bridge opened.	The Watcombe estate extends as Brunel buys more land.

1858	1858
Great Eastern launched.	Arthur James meets Mr and Mrs Brunel "...planning and setting out gardens..."

1859	1859
Torquay Station opened. Royal Albert Bridge opened.	Brunel commissions Dawson to draw up a map of his estate so that it can be sold.

Brunel died at his home in Duke Street, London on September 15th 1859 and was buried in the family grave in Kensal Green Cemetery

CHAPTER 1:
Launching the Watcombe Adventure

Why the Country House?

As a young man, working with his father on the Thames Tunnel, Brunel confided his dreams in his secret journal. He would build ships to storm the pirate lair of Algiers, create bridges and tunnels that would be engineering wonders, and 'at last be rich, have a house built of which I have even made the drawings, be the first engineer and an example to future ones.' Soon afterwards an accident in the tunnel led

The Thames Tunnel painted in 1835 by Sir Marc Brunel who commenced this pioneering feat of engineering. It was soon to become Isambard Kingdom Brunel's first engineering project, as he worked with his father to create the first tunnel in the world under a navigable river. The Victorians referred to it as "The Eighth Wonder of the World". It is still part of the London Underground system. © The Brunel Museum, London

to a long bout of illness and depression. All that could be expected, he told himself, was a mediocre success and an income of £200 or £300 a year. Even that could be bearable, he supposed. 'Get a snug little berth and then a snug little wife with a little somewhat to assist in housekeeping?' These limited aspirations were soon put aside. Ahead of him lay the successes of Clifton Bridge, Bristol Docks and the Great Western Railway. At the end of 1835 he looked back to the times when he was just emerging from the obscurity of unprofitable toil. Now he could tot up the figures: he was engineer to over five million pounds worth of projects, all profitable, sound professional jobs. Some – such as the Cheltenham line - were less welcome; yet 'it's a proud thing to monopolize all the west as I do.'

His professional career established, Brunel could make a start on converting to reality those dreams of his earlier days. He could now afford to leave 53 Parliament Street, where he had founded his fortune, and take a lease of Lord Devon's house at 18 Duke Street, 'a fine house.' Here he could establish not only his office, but also his home. At the age of twenty-one he had doubted whether he could make a good husband: 'my profession is after all my only fit wife…'

1 - Brunel's Duke Street Office, London.   He only had one chair so as to prevent dawdlers and timewasters.

2 - The sofa on which Brunel used to snatch a little sleep.

Portrait of Mary Horsley by her brother John Horsley
Anonymous Collection

Now he was ready to venture on matrimony. 'Mrs B. – I foresee one thing – this time 12 months I shall be a married man. How will that be? Will it make me happier?' No longer was a 'snug little wife' envisaged. Now it was to be the stately Mary Horsley, sister of the artist John Horsley, dubbed by her family 'Duchess of Kensington.'

By 1848 Brunel's position was sufficiently assured for him to purchase the adjoining property - 17, Duke Street. Now he and his family could lead a life of almost aristocratic flamboyance. An inventory of November 1858 gives details of the luxury of the furnishings and fittings: Indian carpets and Venetian glass, organ and grand piano, pictures by leading artists. It was a home over which Mary Brunel could preside with grace and distinction; and here her brother, John Horsley, could enjoy both the noble setting and the music of the beautiful chamber organ, 'that king of musical instruments.' Brunel's biographer, L.T.C. Rolt, suggested that Duke Street 'was not only the symbol of his success but the one stable thing in his restless, hectic life.' This judgement seems too extreme, ignoring the fact that town property, however luxurious, was not the ultimate symbol of worldly success. Mid-Victorian England was the golden age of the country house and of country house society. Successful lawyers, manufacturers, West Indies planters, East India traders – most set the seal on their achievement by becoming a landowner.

Nor were the leading engineers any different: Sir William Armstrong was typical, fitting out 'Cragside' in Northumberland with all the technical advances and conveniences of the new industrial age. To some people engineers were no more than 'rude mechanicals': a letter to the *Times* on 24th November 1846 proclaimed that engineers were 'a useful class of men, but no gentlemen.' Engineers in their country houses, however, were in a position to assert their status as country gentlemen. Some of these new men not only built country palaces but also surrounded them with rolling acres – 'Westonbirt' is a case in point, built by Holford from the profits of London's New River Company. But the fashion by now was not for a country seat but a house in the country, often with less than 100 acres of land surrounding it: Sir James Watts used his fortune from Manchester drapery to build a flamboyant home, 'Abney Hall', but it had only 70 acres of land.

Some of the furnishings that graced Isambard Kingdom Brunel's home at 17 Duke Street, London.
Anonymous Collection

To acquire landed property, then, was a sign of having 'arrived'; but with Brunel two other factors were probably involved. In the first place he was descended from a long line of farmers at Hacqueville in Normandy, stretching back to the 15th Century: it was only the chances of the French Revolution and the subsequent wars that had brought the family to England. Land was in Brunel's blood, and he relished the contact with it derived from his railway work.

That work brought him through some of the loveliest countryside in southern England, stirring in him the urge to possess and shape some of that landscape for himself and his family. But not only the landscape: twenty years earlier he had dreamed of building his own house – had already drawn up some plans.

This was the second factor behind the Watcombe Adventure. It would not be enough to settle in the countryside on an estate built by other men's hands: this must be his own venture, his own dream becoming reality. So it was that on Christmas Eve, 1847, while most men were relaxing by their firesides, Brunel was writing the letter with which the Adventure began. He wrote off for a reference, ('at once if you would'), for a gardener, Alexander Forsyth. His task would be 'to superintend the formation of a park where all is to be done.'

It was probably a few years earlier that Brunel chanced upon this spot that

On Christmas Eve, 1847, while most men were relaxing by their firesides, Brunel was writing off for a reference, ('at once if you would'), for a gardener, Alexander Forsyth. His task would be 'to superintend the formation of a park where all is to be done.' © University of Bristol

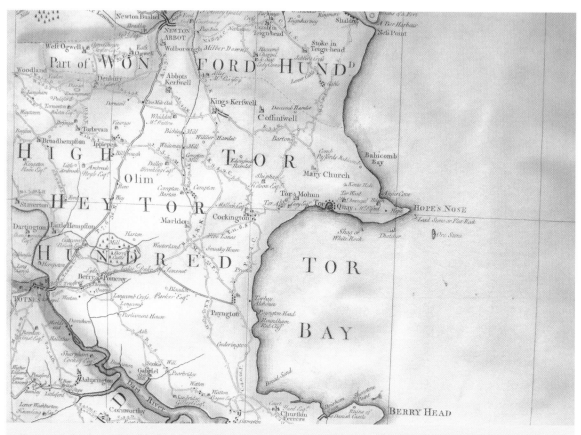

Benjamin Donn's Map of 1765 shows how isolated Torquay was before the building of the Shaldon Bridge and the coming of the railways © Torquay Museum

would be the setting for his future home. He had explored the area when seeking a feasible route for a railway between Teignmouth and Torquay. (None could be found, and the main line ran instead up the north bank of the Teign to Newton Abbot and then along the fringes of Dartmoor to Plymouth. Torquay was served by the branch line to Dartmouth.) In the past this coastal area had been poorly served by roads. Benjamin Donn's Map of Devon, 1765, shows clearly the isolation of Torbay, by-passed by the main routes to the west that led to Plymouth and Falmouth. Most of the local roads remained the steep, narrow and 'cledgey' ways that had plagued William of Orange on his advance from Brixham in 1688. But in 1827 the mouth of the Teign was bridged at Shaldon and

a turnpike road carved along the steep hillsides. For a time this became the main access route to Torquay: along here came the mail coaches, and along here dashed the Brixham fish carts on their way to the London train. And along here came Brunel when railway work brought him this way. After the long climb from Maidencombe the horses needed a breather on the narrow ridge before starting the final descent to Torquay. Here, Brunel's son Isambard tells us, his father used to descend from the coach and walk a little way into the fields. From here he could enjoy a view extending from Berry Head, across the sweep of Torbay and away to the southern slopes of Dartmoor. What a site for a house! Earlier country houses had been built on low ground for the sake of shelter, but this gave little scope for landscape design. Now, with the appearance of the 'Picturesque', men saw the advantages of building high and gaining distant views.

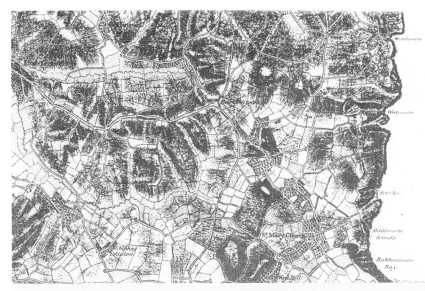

At some time in 1847 Brunel must have taken the plunge, and decided that this was the place for that country home of which he had long dreamed. In many ways it was a bold – probably even a rash – decision. To begin with, he already had another major project in view, the extension of his home and offices in Duke Street; and the times were hardly propitious for estate-building. (It was a time of slump: during the 1840's and 1850's there was a marked decline in the number of new country houses.) It was also the time of economic and political upheaval known as the 'Hungry Forties'. Even Torquay had serious bread riots in June 1847, put down with severity. Two ringleaders were transported, each for ten years; six men were jailed for seven years, and sixty-four for 12 months. In Europe 1848 was the Year of Revolutions. In Britain railway building was in the doldrums and Brunel was laying off, with regret, some of his young engineers. His experimental Atmospheric Railway in South Devon was meeting insoluble problems and would soon be abandoned with heavy losses.

If the economic basis for the Watcombe Adventure was unpromising, so was the proposed site. About the only existing assets were the turnpike road that provided access, and the magnificent

Bathing Machines on Meadfoot Beach. Medical men prescribed Torquay's mild climate and sea-water bathing.

Giant Rock picture © Torquay Museum

Stokeinteignhead and Kingskerswell. Few men, let alone a man with Brunel's range of commitments, would have considered such a project. Most men would have been content to purchase and improve some existing estate. It seems he must have viewed this difficult area as a challenge, much as the Knight family took on the wastes of Exmoor turning bog land into farmland. For Brunel the joy lay in creation more than in possession: in the unpromising surroundings of Watcombe he would build an estate and create a landscape.

Why near Torquay?

At the end of 1835 Brunel prided himself on 'monopolising all the West', and it was in the Bristol area that he found fame and had many friends and supporters. With its attractive countryside, and easy access to London, this might seem a more likely setting for estate-building. Probably it was all too comfortable and over-occupied: by contrast Torbay had all the challenge and excitement of newly-discovered territory. Various factors had brought the area to the forefront. During the long French Wars Torbay had become a frequent - though risky - anchorage for the Royal Navy. (Nelson had predicted that it could one day become its graveyard.) Deprived for a quarter of a century of access to the mild climate of Italy and the French Riviera, invalids and the elderly were in need of a home-grown substitute: hence Torbay's proud claim to be the English Riviera.

views. The area was steep, windswept and waterless, divided by the usual massive Devon hedge banks into an intricate pattern of tiny fields. Land ownership was also complex: the land required for the estate belonged to at least ten different owners, not all readily prepared to sell. There was the added complication that the land straddled three parishes – St. Marychurch,

Medical men prescribed its mild climate and sea-water bathing. Travellers such as Rev. John Swete enthused over the splendour of its setting. He proclaimed that 'a quarry with its ruddy tints crested with a fine edge of wood and the empurpled height of a little mountain beyond finish a picture of unparalleled beauty.' Artists followed suit in romanticizing the limestone cliffs and valleys of the surrounding coastline: in their landscapes the prominent feature of Giant Rock became a formidable crag. Finally the area had the powerful endorsement of royalty. Victoria came as princess in 1833 and fell in love with the setting of Babbacombe where she landed to take tea. In August 1846 she was back as Queen, along with the Prince Consort, and wrote an enthusiastic account of Babbacombe Bay in her journal. 'It is a beautiful spot which before we had only passed at a distance. Red cliffs and rocks with wooded hills like Italy and reminding one of a ballet or play where nymphs appear – such rocks and grottos, with the deepest sea on which there was no ripple.'

The development of Torquay was to some extent stimulated, and to a great degree harmed, by the rivalry of the two great landowning families – Carys and Palks. Carys had been prominent in the area since before the Spanish Armada and dominated much of the countryside. In 1768 they were joined by Robert Palk – his fortune made in the service of the East India Company. He was looked upon very much as an upstart, disturbing old country ways with his plans for commercial development. There was no prospect of co-operation in drawing up a town plan: Torquay developed piecemeal to its future disadvantage. By Brunel's time both families had largely dissipated their energies and their fortunes with their rival schemes of development.

Elegant villas were being laid out on the slopes of Torbay's many hills above the harbour.

In 1848-9 the 15 houses of 'Hesketh Crescent' perched above Meadfoot Beach were built.

By 1846 the Palk family finances were so desperate that land was hurriedly sold to the South Devon Railway to raise £4,000, so that Sir L.V. Palk could escape to France to evade his creditors. A few years later, in 1857 the Cary family home, 'Torre Abbey', became available to rent. *To be LET, Furnished for the Winter Season or longer as may be agreed on, the NOBLE FAMILY MANSION, Torre Abbey, Torquay. Situate in a beautiful timber park and pleasure ground…containing entrance hall, vestibule, large drawing room and dining rooms, library…15 best and 8 servants' bedrooms, servants' hall…stabling for 18 horses and a coach-house for 4 carriages. With every convenience for a large family of distinction.*

Families of distinction were now beating a path to Torquay. As the advertisement makes clear, wintertime was the fashionable time for families to arrive with their servants and carriages. They would settle down in Torre Abbey, or in one of the elegant villas now being laid out on the slopes of Torbay's many hills above the harbour. 'Villa Vomero', an imposing building in Italianate style, was completed in 1838: and in 1848-9 came the 15 houses of 'Hesketh Crescent' perched above Meadfoot Beach. Soon the *Torquay Directory* would list the nobility and minor royalty – British and foreign – inhabiting such places: and both 'Vomero' and 'Hesketh Crescent' provided temporary accommodation for Brunel as he set out upon his Watcombe Adventure. Torquay swiftly became less fashionable and less adventurous.

By 1864, when Trollope published *The Small House at Allington*, Torquay provided a suitable setting for Bernard Dale's parents – 'an effete, invalid, listless couple, pretty well dead to all the world beyond the region of the Torquay card-tables.' The town's stuffy character was noted by Disraeli and Landor; while – a little later – Kipling was seized by an impish urge to upset the place 'by dancing through it with nothing on but my spectacles.'

So swiftly did Torquay become dull and characterless: but in Brunel's time it possessed all the slightly raffish excitement of a frontier town. The Census figures show how rapid was the growth, and how the expansion sucked in men and women not only from the West Country but from far and wide. (The population of St. Marychurch was 2293 in 1851 – an increase of 525 in the past ten years: by 1861 its population had doubled!) Local newspapers of the time provide a flavour of this teeming, unstable society: on one side a luxurious life-style; on the other the 'huddled masses' of Torquay's cholera-ridden slums. In the 1840's and 1850's Torquay welcomed such notables as the Dowager Queen Adelaide, ex-Queen Marie of France and the Duchess of Orleans: Bulwer Lytton, Charles Kingsley and Philip Gosse came here to develop their literary and scientific talents. Characteristic of this 'new society' of Torquay was the friendship between the wealthy philanthropist, Baroness Burdett-Coutts, and William Pengelly, self-taught son of a Cornish mariner, whose researches in local caverns established the antiquity of man. Typical of the 'new men' who were forming Torquay was Edward Vivian, son of a Hertfordshire squire. Like Queen Victoria he first saw the area from the sea and determined to make his home there. He joined the Palk family's agent, William Kitson, in founding the Torbay Bank in 1833 – Brunel's West Country bankers. Vivian became the leading figure in many local enterprises, such as

the founding of the Natural History Society with its museum in 1844.

Other activities than card-playing and Natural History had drawn people to the town. The presence of the Royal Navy in Napoleonic times had seen the first primitive regattas, and this enterprise became Royal, with Victoria's gracious consent, in 1839. In 1851 came an intrusive challenger from the New York Yacht Club, the schooner *America*, which ran rings round the local craft. In that same year, 1851, the Torquay Cricket Club was founded – perhaps the most important sign of all that Torquay had 'arrived'. And now people could come to Torquay, not only by sea or by the still inadequate roads, but by train. On 15th December 1848, almost exactly a year after Brunel wrote off about the gardener who was to form his park, the South Devon Railway brought the first train to Torre Station.

In the late 1840's, then, Brunel came to a town and society that would today be described as 'vibrant', and that would be transformed ever faster through the arrival of the railway. He was coming to Devon to share the excitement of a boom town – not to bury himself away in some form of retirement ghetto. This was entirely in keeping with so many aspects of his professional and private life: his ambition to extend his Great Western Railway to New York; his risky climbing venture in Clifton Gorge; his leadership of a private army of 2,000 navvies at the Battle of Mickleton Tunnel. It was typical

The Opening of Torre Station, Torquay on 15th December 1848
© Torquay Museum

of Brunel's 'adventurism' that in April and May 1848 - at a time when he was heavily involved, both with his Duke Street plans and with the purchase of his Watcombe estate - he 'took off' with brother-in-law John Horsley on an extended visit to France to attend Republican meetings and buy furniture. Living dangerously was meat and drink to Brunel, and Watcombe was yet another of his adventures.

Brunel builds up his Team

As with his engineering work, Brunel showed great capacity to make use of other men's talents. As noted earlier, it was on Christmas Eve 1847 that he sought information on Alexander Forsyth who was to become his estate manager. Like many leading gardeners of the day he was a Scotsman of talent, and had worked for the Earl of Shrewsbury at

Alton Towers. In 1842 he had married a Teignmouth girl, Anne Burgess, which may well account for his wish to move to Devon. Having secured his man Brunel moved fast. There were as yet no houses on the planned estate, so by February 1848 Forsyth had moved down with his family and was housed at '3, Park Crescent' in the nearby parish of St. Marychurch. (There are some interesting and unusual trees in the garden, so Forsyth may well have brought some stock down with him.) By the time of the 1851 Census he had moved to one of a pair of newly-built cottages, now forming the rear portion of 'Brunel Lodge' at the top of Maidencombe Hill. There he was well-placed to supervise his teams as they progressed with the planting of Brunel's trees along the hillsides. There he drank his favourite beverage of holly-leaf tea, and composed occasional quirky letters to the local press and professional journals.

Brunel was only forty-one when he began work at Watcombe. His plan was to purchase land, develop the estate and form the surrounding landscape long before he began to build his house. Because he was so often away from the area, he chose his local agents with care. His surveyor and land agent was William Dawson of 7, Northernhay Place, Exeter, who later worked closely with Brunel on railway development. Brunel's solicitors were Sanders and Kitson of Exeter, who had much work to do in sorting out complex land deals. Finance was dealt with by Drummond's Bank in London, and local payments by Vivian and Kitson's Bank in Torquay. The whole operation was closely supervised by Brunel himself, and by his conscientious Secretary, Joseph Bennett, from 18 Duke Street in London. The letters sent out from Duke Street between 1847 and 1859 tell part of the story of how Brunel became a landowner, how closely he became involved in local affairs, and how he created a landscape that largely survives today.

It is a story that is treated as no more than a side-issue by Brunel's foremost biographer, L.T.C. Rolt. Watcombe is seen as a plaything for his few idle moments, as a dream world that faded away behind the realities of his struggle with the *Great Eastern*. Yet the letters confirm that Brunel handled his Watcombe venture with the same enterprise, professionalism and creative enthusiasm that he showed in his engineering. For twelve years he worked away, buying up land, laying down roads, digging wells and – above all – planting trees. The first letter concerning land purchase was written to Dawson in Exeter on 27th January, 1848. 'Drummonds will tomorrow pay into Barclay and Co. to your account at the Exeter Bank £2,926.17.0, being the amount mentioned in your letter which is to be paid this week for certain lands purchased by Mr. Brunel.' (Signed J. Bennett) This was followed by other letters disclosing Brunel's personal and enthusiastic interest. By April 7th he was

writing to Dawson about his plans for pumping water to the high ground where he proposed, eventually, to build his house. In a postscript he displayed that attention to precise detail that marked all his planning. 'In setting out the new road marked C.D. on your last sketch, take care to keep it as clear as possible of the trees at the extreme North corner of no. 83 & between that and 82 – that is to keep the road so far North as to leave as many of these to the North of the road as you can – a few feet will make the difference.'

It was as well that Brunel could rely upon the diligent Bennett to take charge of his affairs. In April and May 1848, as already mentioned, Citoyen Brunel was flirting with French republicanism in Paris. So it was Bennett to whom the task fell of dealing with Sanders and Kitson over the delicate matter of the purchase money – amounting to £5845 – for a large block of land purchased from Henry Langford Brown of 'Barton Hall', Kingskerswell. (Fortunately for Brunel Langford Brown was a yachting enthusiast, and was willing to sell almost any amount of land to finance his hobby.) Bennett first wrote on May 8th, saying that Mr. Brunel would deal with the matter on his return. He wrote again on May 19th saying that Mr. Brunel would not be able to arrange payment until the end of the following week. A week later, on May 26th, he wrote that it would be 'rather awkward' for Mr. Brunel to make payment 'except on completion and execution of the Deeds as Mr Brunel is so situated that it would be very unpleasant for him to have any point of difficulty arising with any parties down in Devonshire.' Without a doubt this concern to avoid any fresh problems was due to the increasing difficulties with the ill-fated Atmospheric Railway. It was in August that the decision was taken to abandon the system, and Brunel then declined to draw more than a nominal salary until the line was completed to Plymouth in April 1849. (He had also suffered a major financial loss from the collapse of the company that owned *Great Britain* following the heavy cost of salvage and repairs following its grounding.)

There are further signs in the letters of temporary financial embarrassment. Various payments for land were made between 1st June and 1st August, and Dawson was paid £200 for his land agency work. But payment for a second purchase of land from Brown was postponed on 4th August and again on 25th August. 'Mr Brunel desires me to say that it will not be possible to make it until the week after next. You will no doubt remember that payment was understood to be postponed until it was convenient for Mr. Brunel to make it.' On that very same day Brunel, with great reluctance, dismissed twelve engineers: across the country railway companies had gone bankrupt or suspended work. As always Brunel came to a bold decision: he would continue his estate-building at this time of financial crisis, and when already heavily committed at Duke Street. This disruption at his London property, together with the need for close attention to Watcombe, was probably the reason why Torquay became his base for much of the summer and autumn. The *Torquay Directory* recorded Mr and Mrs Brunell and Family (mis-spelt with double ll) as being at the magnificent villa, 'The Vomero', from July 12th until November 22nd. This imposing residence overlooking Torbay provided a comfortable and convenient forward base for Brunel's work, much of which was now in the West Country. During this extended stay in Torquay he could give close attention to his programme of road-building. (The first recorded payment of £40 to his gardener, Forsyth, was on 4th August.)

Villa Vomero. Isambard Kingdom Brunel stayed here with his wife and family from July 12th until November 22nd 1848 as he worked on the railways and began to establish the founding his Watcombe Estate © Viewpoint Designs

CHAPTER 2:
Landowning has its Problems

Trouble over the Parish Roads

A further reason for Brunel being on the spot was possibly to counter some serious opposition to his proposals - especially over the matter of re-aligning the local road network. To allow for the laying out of his estate it would be crucial to secure the closure of the old parish road from St. Marychurch to Stokeinteignhead. The construction of the turnpike road from Teignmouth had created an improved route, providing an opportunity that Brunel's practised eye was quick to notice. Driving along that coast road one can still spot three

On the south side, the old Teignmouth road sweeps down the hillside alongside Brunel's now overgrown romantic water features and through the woods he planted to form his Green Lane vista   Image: Tracey Elliot-Reep

To the north of Brunel's estate, the old road can still be seen closed off with a gate
Image: Tracey Elliot-Reep

sections where the old parish roads climbed the hills and dipped into the valleys with breakneck gradients: the turnpike builders skirted around the hilltops and cut into the side of ridges to provide a considerably longer but easier route. Before reaching the summit of the Maidencombe ridge there is a fourth section of overgrown lane, now closed off with a gate. This rose steeply to the summit, then plunged even more steeply into the narrow valley leading to Watcombe.

This valley was to be the heartland of Brunel's estate, with his house and garden at the top, his park and woodland stretching away below. Before purchasing any land Brunel must have taken

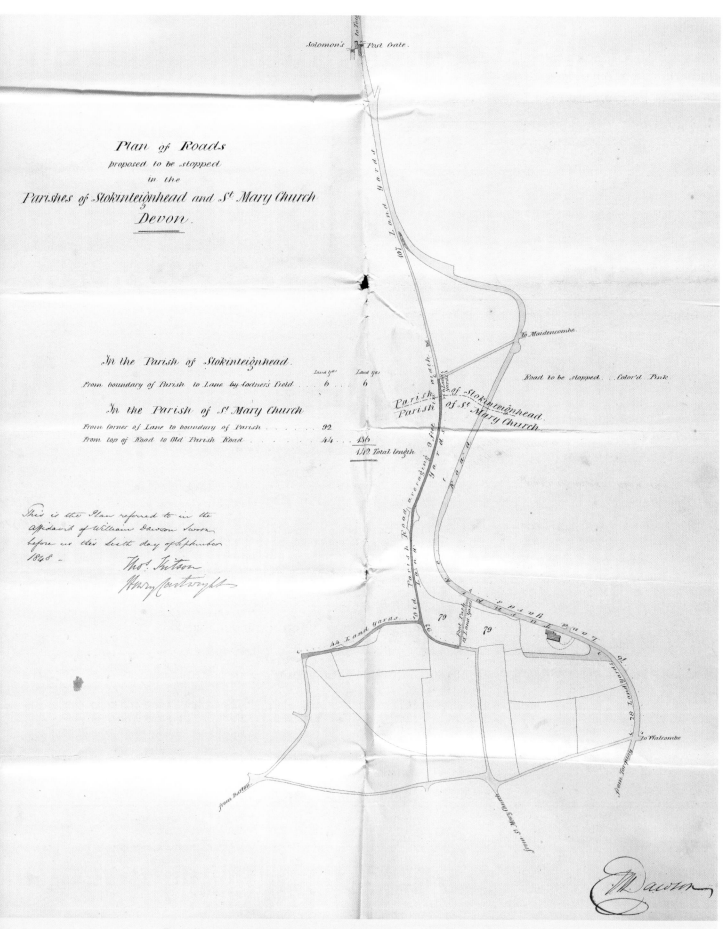

Plan of Roads
proposed to be stopped
in the
Parishes of Stokinteignhead and S.t Mary Church
Devon.

Solomon's Post Gate.

In the Parish of Stokinteignhead.

	Land yd.s	Land yd.s
From boundary of Parish to Lane by Godner's Field	6	6

In the Parish of S.t Mary Church

From corner of Lane to boundary of Parish		92
From top of Road to Old Parish Road	44	136
		142 Total length

Parish of Stokinteignhead
Parish of S.t Mary Church

Road to be stopped. Color'd Pink

to Maidencombe.

to Walcombe

This is the Plan referred to in the
Affidavit of William Dawson Sworn
before us this Sixth day of September
1848 —

Tho.s Tutson
Henry Cartwright

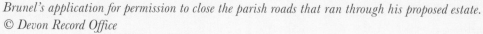

Brunel's application for permission to close the parish roads that ran through his proposed estate.
© Devon Record Office

soundings and assured himself that there was unlikely to be strong opposition from landowners and parishes concerned. The turnpike provided a better route for through traffic, and some accommodation could be provided for local users. So Brunel's surveyor went to work to draw up the necessary plans and documents for Devon Quarter Sessions to consider and approve: Brunel's local friends and allies sought to ensure that the proposal would receive the assent of St. Marychurch Vestry – the body then responsible for parish roads. Here Brunel's plans seem to have met unexpected opposition. Strong local feelings must have become involved, because the Vestry attendance was much higher than usual when it met on 17th June, 1848. Fourteen members attended: 'the Meeting proceeded to read the notice of Mr. Brunel; and also the report of the committee appointed to assist the Surveyor of the Highways – which was to the effect that the proposed change would not be advisable.'

Here was a major upset. No road closure - no possibility of laying out Watcombe Park. Fortunately for Brunel his friends and allies must have been prepared for this challenge. Rev. Thomas Kitson (brother of Brunel's banker and a local magistrate) would have realised that a prolonged wrangle might well prove fatal to Brunel's plans. He moved that the report be received, thus cutting short any debate, and the meeting was promptly adjourned for a week. Faced with this crisis, Brunel must have dropped

The Torquay Directory of 28th June 1848 recorded that Mr and Mrs Brunel and their son Isambard were staying at Webb's Royal Hotel.
© *Torquay Museum*

everything and hurried down to Torquay to set matters straight. *The Torquay Directory* of 28th June recorded that Mr and Mrs Brunel and their son Isambard were staying at Webb's Royal Hotel. They must have arrived some days earlier to sort out this problem over the roads, and Brunel may even have attended the Vestry Meeting on 24th June in person. He knew his Devon folk. Earlier that year he had told a meeting in Plymouth that 'he knew of no county in England where falsehood grew so wonderfully or prevailed so extensively as in Devon.' No doubt rumours of all kinds had spread around St. Marychurch about this assault on the local roads: the skills of advocacy and persuasion that Brunel exercised so successfully upon Parliamentary Committees may perhaps have helped to win over this Devon Vestry.

Brunel agreed to construct this pathway and steps for the pedestrian right of way to the turnpike road, fulfilling the terms the St. Marychurch Vestry made when they consented to the road closures for his estate. Image: Helen Hillard

During the interval between the meetings steps must have been taken to persuade opponents, to reassure waverers, and to wrap the whole proposal in the wholesome cloak of legality. Apart from making concessions on his proposals, Brunel also undertook to give employment to local men and carts, an important incentive at a time of economic depression. The proposal was now written into the Vestry Minutes at length, and the substituted highway was specified in detail – running through fields bearing the pleasant-sounding names of Holloway, The Great Park, Woodsberry and Peaseland. The Chairman, Rev. William Maskell, resolved that it was expedient that these various changes should be made, 'and

that the inhabitants now here assembled do agree to the same…' The resolution concluded that all expenses were to be repaid to the Surveyor of the Highways 'by Isambard Kingdom Brunel as the Statute in that behalf directs.' The Chairman could now sign an order to the Surveyor, Samuel Taylor, which set the whole legal procedure for road closure in motion. Brunel could breathe freely again. On 10th July he signed a brief 'Consent' by which he agreed to construct a pathway and steps at his own expense and through his own lands 'in consideration of the Land and Soil of the old highways coloured pink in the said plan being vested in me…'

Two weeks later, on 22nd July, the proposed road changes were viewed by two local magistrates, Rev. Thomas Kitson and Henry Cartwright Esq. and the Surveyors trudged up the hillsides to fix the statutory notices by the side and at each end of the roads affected. The next day, 23rd July, notices were fixed to the church door both at Stokeinteignhead and St. Marychurch: later the Surveyors certified that these notices had remained there for three further Sundays. To provide the required wider notice the proposal was advertised during four successive weeks in *Trewman's Flying Post*. The way was now clear for the two magistrates to carry out the final steps. On 6th September they verified Dawson's plan of the road changes and all the other documents involved, and then drew up a detailed three-page certificate to be set before Devon

Quarter Sessions on 17th October. This confirmed that all legal requirements had been met; and also certified that the old roads were unnecessary and useless because they were narrow and steep, and that 'better and more commodious communication between the Termini of the said Highways is afforded by adjoining wide and open roads…' Now nearly all was done that had to be done. The next day the papers were lodged with the Clerk of the Peace in Exeter who drew up a list to check that all the documents were in order: (he missed out the notice affixed to the St. Marychurch church door.) Quarter Sessions took place on 17th October: the closure order was confirmed and written into the Order Book. All the legal formalities were now completed. Brunel must have been itching to make a start: £100 was sent down to Dawson in November 'towards the new roads,' and a further £100 in December.

Brunel showed no inclination to pile acre upon acre, accumulating land solely for its prestige value: all of his purchases were strictly for a purpose. Securing the closure of the old parish roads safeguarded two elements of the proposed estate – the site of the house at the head of the valley, and the land for gardens and arboretum falling away beneath it towards the distant view of Torbay. Behind the house site the ridge levelled out to form a small plateau, providing space for gardeners' cottages and greenhouses, stables and kitchen garden. A further narrow strip of land beyond these was needed for the planting of a shelter-belt to provide protection from northerly gales.

These were the bare essentials, but some further land-purchases were desirable. Away to the north-west the ridge climbed gently towards the summit of Great Hill to join the road to Newton Abbot: gaining this land would provide the most direct – and the most spectacular – approach to the estate. Away to the south, beyond the arboretum, lay the flat ground of the Watcombe clay beds: there, Brunel felt certain, was the source of the estate's water supply. In both these areas the required land was purchased. One further stretch of land caught Brunel's eye and was added to the estate as funds became available. This was the hilly ground to the east, between the Teignmouth road and the sea. Owning this land was perhaps a luxury rather than a necessity: it provided further space for tree-planting, together with the bonus of far-reaching views across Lyme Bay.

The conversion of farmland into parkland required more than the creation of new roads. The vast amount of earth moving involved was noted by a local lad, William Grant, and recorded seventy years later when he wrote his Memoirs in the 1920's. (He complained that he felt the writing rather arduous at his age, but happily he stuck to the task.) Grant was twelve when Brunel came to Watcombe, twenty-three when Brunel died; and his account has the vivid detail of one who has seen it all happen. There was…'fencing and clearing the ground, pulling up hedges and trees and all encumbrance, after a short time there were fifty men employed. Many horses with carts removing earth from one part to another, also carting peat from Milber Down, about four miles away, thousands of cart-loads were, I believe, taken from there.' Presumably this initial clearance was carried out by the local labour-force, but gangs of railway navvies under a Mr. Cogswell were later employed on the skilled work of constructing the hedge-banks to line Brunel's new roads. These were formed using methods developed by Brunel during his railway construction. The

stonework was so arranged that the weight held the bank inwards rather than – as in many Devon hedge-banks – tending to push it outwards. After a century and a half these banks of Brunel's remain like military fortifications, erect and almost undamaged. Another example of Brunel's painstaking approach was in the construction of the carriage drives carved into the hillsides. These were wide and substantial enough for the passage of light carriages to viewpoints, where there was seating and provision for turning. The outside edges of these drives were lined with a band of pebbles to provide

Examples of the pebble-edged trackways that weave through Brunel's estate
Images: Tracey Elliot-Reep (right) & Helen Hillard (left)

additional strength and stability: collecting and transporting these matched pebbles from their beach source must have been laborious and costly. It was worth the trouble. Despite years of neglect these drives remain largely unimpaired while more recent pathways are sliding away down the steep hillsides.

More Land – and more Problems

So many parcels of land were being purchased that even the meticulous Bennett became confused at times. In September he sought confirmation from the Exeter solicitors that all the land had in fact been paid for; in November there was confusion over Forsyth's estate accounts; and in January 1849 all remaining deeds were rushed up to London because of a sudden panic. A recent serious fire in Lincoln's Inn had destroyed a large number of legal documents, and now Brunel was anxious lest the evidence of his estate-building should disappear in smoke and ashes. On 17th January, he wrote to Sanders & Kitson: 'I enclose you a cheque for £250 and shall feel obliged at your discharging Mr. Coleridge's account – and will you also send me yours – and after the fearful fire in Lincoln's Inn I feel anxious to know whether I have all the deeds connected with my purchase and if not to request that you will have the goodness to send them up that I may put them in a safe place – as you may have a blaze in Exeter as well as here and I have an intense horror of any trouble or confusion in such matters.'

This affair provides an interesting insight into Brunel's personality, and also demonstrates the great importance to him of this land-ownership. When he moved on a matter like this he moved fast. The very next day Brunel's London solicitor was summoned to Duke Street to receive all the documents already in Brunel's possession. The solicitor and his clerks must have spent a busy day checking all the documents; and then he was back again in the evening for a further discussion about listing 'all the documents you should have in all the 6 purchases.' Next morning he was back once more at Duke Street, checking and listing further documents sent up from Exeter by Kitson, and 'drawing out list of further papers and documents which we considered should have been sent up by Mr. Kitson or the want of them explained, and attending Mr. Bennett therewith and he was to write to Mr. Kitson thereon.' Poor Bennett must have been uncomfortably placed, between Brunel – who wanted all the papers safely deposited in Drummond's Bank the very next day, January 20th – and the solicitor who insisted on further checking.

It was not until January 22nd that Bennett was able to send across the box of papers for more listing and scheduling. It must have been a relief to all concerned when at last, on January 23rd, the solicitor was able to hand over the whole collection to the Clerk at Drummond's Bank, ('engaged two hours.') Two days later the receipt and

The far end of Brunel's Great Hill Driveway
Image: Tracey Elliot-Reep

accomplished in just seven days and cost Brunel £2 3s 4d – along with an extra 1s 6d for the porter who carried the box. The legal basis of Brunel's Watcombe Adventure now lay safely in the vaults of Drummond's Bank, and Brunel's head presumably rested more easily on his pillow. (But not for long. Brunel was now a man of property, and he spent seven months – from January to June 1849 – at the complex task of drawing up his will.)

With the safe deposit of the property deeds the first year of Brunel's estate-building was successfully concluded, but he was soon hard at work developing the land and making fresh purchases. In January 1849 Brunel sent down £1,600 to his Torquay account with Vivian and Kitson, and in April and May he was negotiating with Mr Beasley of Torquay over the insurance of a house at Watcombe: '…it will be some time before

the key of the box were handed over to Mr. Bennett, who was no doubt glad to be able to resume his normal duties. All this legal hustle had been

Torbay View from Great Hill   Image: Tracey Elliot-Reep

Lyme Bay View from Great Hill   Image: Tracey Elliot-Reep

I have any new buildings to insure at Mary Church.' By now Brunel and his wife Mary were spending a considerable part of their time in Torquay – in January and February they attended no less than three fancy dress balls at Webb's Royal Hotel, Brunel being listed as one of the Stewards. There were five further visits to Webb's Hotel during the Spring and Summer – a critical time both for road-building and for further land purchases. In June and July Brunel was involved with the lay-out of the new roads, and then he began negotiating for the purchase of two strips of Admiralty land. These lay at Great Hill, 550 ft., one of the commanding heights around Torbay.

This proposed purchase had its problems. Great Hill was then known –

temporarily – as Telegraph Hill. It had been purchased by the Admiralty around 1825 as the proposed site for one of a chain of Popham semaphore stations linking London with Plymouth. As with most present-day projects costs escalated, and at a time of British naval supremacy and world peace there was no pressure to prepare for war. By 1849 the electric telegraph was in being and a long-distance visual signalling system was obsolete. So the land was to be sold back to the original owners, Brown and Collins, and Brunel was concerned about this. He insisted that the land should be conveyed direct to him, rather than re-conveyed by the original owners: '…I have particular reasons, quite apart from the expense, for wishing to have it direct from the Crown.' He suggested putting his Exeter solicitors directly in touch with the Admiralty Solicitor, Mr. Robson, 'who I know will facilitate matters.' We can only speculate on Brunel's 'particular reasons' for wishing to arrange matters in this way. Possibly it was simply that, still smarting from his earlier dealings with the Admiralty, he had a dread of the transactions falling into bureaucratic thickets and disappearing without trace. Possibly he had wind of some other potential purchaser. In the event Brunel gained his objective, as minuted in Admiralty records: September 4th, 1849, 'Great Hill sold to Mr. Brunel for £10.' Considering the importance of the land to Brunel he had secured a bargain.

This land across Great Hill would form Brunel's most important access route and much of his land-purchasing was designed to safeguard it. Even before securing the Admiralty land he had arranged through his solicitors that Mr.

H.L. Brown, owner of Barton Hall had transferred to Mr. Brunel 'his interest in the road leading to the great hill.' Along it, to begin with, came those thousands of cart loads of peat to prepare the ground for tree-planting. Eventually this land would provide a spectacular approach to the Watcombe estate.

A visitor would travel by carriage from Newton Abbot up the Milber ridge and along the Keyberry Turnpike - then one of the few approaches to Torquay. Before reaching Barton, Brunel's driveway would strike off on the old ridgeway across Great Hill, and then descend the eastern slopes towards Watcombe Park. From the ridge there would be spectacular views across Torbay on one side, over to Dartmoor on the other. This was in accord with the new fashion in landscape design. The earlier formal avenues were now out of favour, replaced by less formal, sinuous driveways,

Dartmoor View from Great Hill   Image: Tracey Elliot-Reep

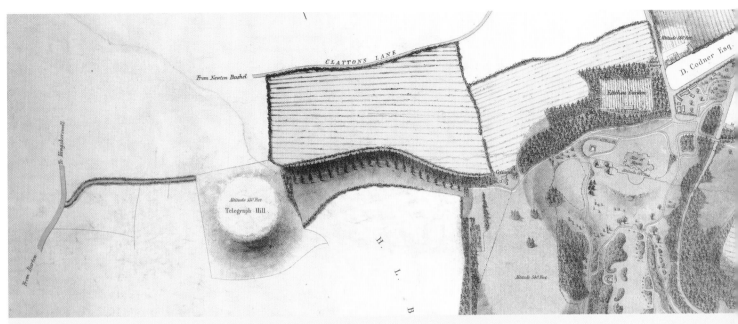

Section of estate Map of 1859 showing Great Hill driveway and lodge   © Devon Record Office

following the contours of the ground.
(One of the longest, a three-mile avenue
of limes, was laid out at Clumber Park in
1840.) A driveway of this kind requires a
lodge, and one was provided, (shown on
the estate map), at the entrance to the
arboretum. It lasted to within living
memory, though its final use was to
house pigs – typical of the sad fate of so
much of Brunel's handiwork at
Watcombe. When finally demolished its
stones were used to build retaining walls
in a nearby garden, though parts of
Brunel's entrance walling are still
standing to provide evidence of this
planned approach.

The Need for a
West Country Base

At the end of the letter to his solicitors
about Great Hill Brunel added the
significant sentence: 'I am anxious to
hear about Watcombe.' This resembled
the concern of a parent for a newly-born

child: clearly he was now deeply involved,
both financially and emotionally, in his
estate, and could not administer it
effectively from Torquay hotels.

His professional life was also extremely
busy: his railway line to Plymouth had
been completed in April and he was now
concerned with the Millbay Docks.
Big challenges lay ahead with the
massive bridges at Chepstow and Saltash
and the complex extension of the railway
line to Penzance. Bridging the Tamar
was probably Brunel's greatest
engineering challenge. He had been
appointed Engineer to the Cornwall
Railway Company after it had secured
Parliamentary consent for a line
between Plymouth and Falmouth in
August 1846. Proposals for a steam train
ferry and two forms of wooden bridge
were rejected by the Admiralty,
concerned that its full use of the estuary
should not be impeded. In conclusion the
Admiralty stipulated that there should
not be more than one pier in the fairway,

and that there should be a minimum height of 100 feet above high water.

In response to these requirements Brunel produced his design for a wrought iron bridge, with two long spans across the river supported by a central pier. It was 1848 before Admiralty consent was obtained, and much of the year was spent in exploring the bed of the Tamar to discover how to support that central pier. A huge cylinder, 85 feet long, was lowered into the river 35 times, and 175 rock borings were made. These showed that the rock could support the weight of a pier, but to prove his point Brunel built some trial masonry on a portion of the rock. Incorporated in the stonework was a copper plate with the inscription: *Cornwall Railway, Saltash Bridge, Trial Foundation of Central Pier, January 1849, I.K. Brunel, Engineer, William Glennie, Resident Engineer.* In the event, because of financial problems, it was 1852 before work began on bridge construction; but this coming challenge was probably one of the factors persuading Brunel of the need to secure a more substantial base in the West Country that would serve him until his house was built at Watcombe. For a time there was discussion about opening a West Country office in Exeter: presumably the renting of a house obviated the need.

Other factors were involved. Within the family Brunel's father, Marc Brunel, was moving slowly to the death that came in December 1849. (This intimation of mortality was possibly a further reason why Brunel spent from January to June this year in drawing up his will.) From time to time he visited Watcombe, and after a visit in July he wrote to his land agent, Dawson, about the line of a new road. This road affected the interests of a neighbour, Daniel Woodley, owner of the St. Marychurch marble works. There had been some misunderstandings about whether the road was to be built straight or crooked, and whether it was to be a public road. This was the first of a series of entanglements with Woodley and other neighbours that brought home to Brunel that land-ownership had its pitfalls as well as its pleasures.

These recurrent problems – along with the challenge of the Tamar - perhaps convinced Brunel that if there were to be a base it should be close to his property. In August 1849 he became the tenant of 'Watcombe Villa' (now 'Watcombe Lodge') alongside the Teignmouth turnpike. Considerable work must have been required on the house, because in 1850 the Brunels spent three months - between 7th August and 6th November – in temporary accommodation, first at '4, Hesketh Crescent', then at '14, Hesketh Crescent'. ('Temporary accommodation' is perhaps an inadequate description of this splendid array of fifteen houses in Regency style, overlooking Meadfoot Beach. Completed as recently as 1848-9 by the Harvey bothers – Torquay's leading builders – they were inhabited by well-off visitors. As with 'The Vomero' two years earlier, this would certainly have classed as 'a good address.')

As for 'Watcombe Villa', this house seems to have been kept fully-staffed, and was occupied by the family on and off throughout the year. For Brunel it provided a forward base from which he could supervise his West Country projects: for Mary Brunel it was a home from which she could emerge to glitter at the Regatta and New Year Balls. Apart from these distinguished occasions, many reports in the local paper show the extent to which the family became involved with the life of the area. In July 1855, for instance, both Brunel and his wife attended a Grand Fete at Bradley Woods, Newton Abbot, their names appearing among a long list of the great and the good. (An attraction at the Fete

Watcombe Villa (now Watcombe Lodge) - Brunel rented this property, adjacent to his developing estate, 1849 - 1857.
He built the conservatory, constructing it as a model for the glass roof and drainage arrangements for Paddington station.
Image: Helen Hillard

In 1850 the Brunels spent three months - between 7th August and 6th November – in temporary accommodation, first at '4, Hesketh Crescent', then at '14, Hesketh Crescent'. ('Temporary accommodation' is perhaps an inadequate description of this splendid array of fifteen houses in Regency style, overlooking Meadfoot Beach) © Torquay Museum

was a display of models, including the *Great Britain* and Windsor Castle – the former probably created by Brunel.) There were regular contributions to local good works. Mrs Brunel was patron of a Bazaar for Upton Church Spire; contributed a guinea to the Torquay Homeopathic Dispensary; subscribed £1 for food for 'Navvies' and 10/ for 'Widow Roose'. Brunel himself was a regular subscriber to the Regatta Fund, made a donation of £5 to the South Devon Rifle Battalion, and offered £100 towards the cost of an improved water supply at St. Marychurch. From time to time 'Watcombe Villa' was used for

entertaining. *The Torquay Directory* of 1st October 1851 recorded that: 'Benjamin Hawes, Esq., M.P., Under Secretary of State for the Colonies, has been staying for several weeks past with Mr. and Mrs. Brunel at Watcombe. Last week he visited the emigration depot and other public establishments at Plymouth and the prisons on Dartmoor.' (Ben Hawes was Brunel's brother-in-law and one of his closest companions – so this was a family rather than an official visit.)

The Brunels continued to rent 'Watcombe Villa' until the owners sold the property in 1857. To a considerable extent Brunel was now in a position to provide 'hands-on' management of his Watcombe estate: hence from July 1849 to September 1850 there are no major developments recorded in the Letterbooks. There is a sense of work proceeding steadily. Money was sent regularly to Forsyth for wages, together with additional sums for the builder and blacksmith, (staff cottages were being built at this time.) Some of the land was being farmed – money was paid to C. Lawrence for sheep and hurdles, and the local paper recorded that Mr. Brunel was fattening up sheep for the Christmas market. (Not such a strange event for a man descended from a long line of tenant farmers in Normandy.) This seems to have been a period of consolidation – and also of settlement of accounts. Dawson was paid two sums of £100 towards his charges against the Marychurch property, and on 13th July 1850 came the reckoning with Sanders and Kitson for all the legal work involved - £500. Perhaps the clearest indication of progress in estate building was the appearance of a series of 'puffs' in local newspapers when neighbouring property was up for sale. The first of these appeared as early as 19th

Portland Villa, later part of the Maidencombe House Hotel.. The Brunels moved here when Watcombe Villa was sold in 1857 and the family continued to use it even after IKB died in 1859. A plaque now commemorates that he lived on this site, now completely rebuilt as an apartment block.   Post card

September, 1849: **'Titterland Villa',
Watcombe, adjoins tastefully laid out
grounds & site of the about to be
erected Mansion for Isambard
Kingdom Brunel.'** In July 1850 it was
**'Orestone Villa'…adjoining the lands
which Mr. I.K.Brunel has selected to
construct a mansion & domain for**
his own residence.' By 1856 'Portland
Villa', soon to be home to the Brunels, was
advertised as **adjoining beautiful
grounds of Isambard Kingdom Brunel**,
and another villa was described as being
within **'a few minutes walk'** of his
grounds. (As in our own times there was a
certain cachet in living close to a celebrity.)

A plaque now commemorates that he lived on this site, now completely rebuilt as an apartment block.

CHAPTER 3:
Planning the Enterprise

A Water Supply for Watcombe Park

During these early years there is little or no record of what could be termed gardening or tree-planting expenses. (Payment of an account to Veitch, the West Country nurserymen, is recorded on 19th January, 1849. There are no further records of dealings with Veitch in the Bristol Letterbooks – subsequent purchases must have been handled locally.) Much of the time was certainly spent in laying out roads and constructing essential buildings. Alexander Forsyth must have been busy setting-up his 'empire' to the rear of his new cottage. A collection of hothouses was established, as described in subsequent articles in *The Gardeners' Chronicle*, (July 15th 1882 and October 15th 1887), and there was a walled fruit and kitchen garden of three acres. By 1854 Forsyth was sufficiently established to act as Judge at the Torbay Horticultural Society's Exhibitions in June and September. Before large-scale planting could be carried out it was essential to secure an adequate water-supply, and the first indication of this came in September 1850. When he needed help Brunel sought out an acknowledged expert, and he now approached the firm of William Simpson

Page from the back of Brunel's Watcombe Garden Book showing lists of trees planted along the sea walk, first measured in 1849. These measurements and those of 1850 must have been recorded elsewhere and copied into the book in 1853. © *University of Bristol*

of Pimlico, specialist water engineers. A Mr. Thompson of the firm came down to explore the site and consider the options. The choice lay between a very deep well at the top of the hill, or a series of shallow wells at the foot of the valley where Brunel was optimistic he would find 'a great abundance of water.' He now sought from Simpson a comparative estimate of the cost of the two modes of supply. If the valley solution were to be chosen the circumstances would be: 'a lift of 300ft. a distance of 800 yards to the reservoir With a good supply of water at 10 or 12

One of Brunel's original seven wells at the lower end of his estate. Several others have survived. Image: Tracey Elliot-Reep

ft. below the surface of the ground – and if a 5 horse power be assumed in the one case I think we should assume 8 horse in the second – probably the same engine but worked up to a little higher power – I presume that a three and a half or three and three-quarters main would do - but of this you are the judge.'

Presumably investigations and planning continued, but nothing seems to have been done for nearly a year. In the meantime Brunel was heavily engaged with the Great Exhibition of 1851, and also with his brilliant design for Paddington Station. ('...the matter presses very much, the building must be half finished by the summer.') It was not until 1st August 1851 that another letter to Simpson appears, dealing with pumps and the design of engine-houses. Clearly Brunel had gone for the valley solution. The estate map of 1859 shows that he linked seven wells with an adit: this fed two reservoirs – one of them for the benefit of the local inhabitants. To provide power for the pumping a primitive gas engine was installed, as described many years later by Henry Grant of St. Marychurch. 'I saw the engine many times – it was composed of a cylinder at the bottom for the explosion of gas – a steel bar standing perpendicular with ratchets on two sides of the square bar – the gas explosion would instantly raise this heavy bar about six feet high and when at its height would catch into another prepared bar, when it would gradually

Brunel was heavily engaged with the Great Exhibition of 1851   © Elton Collection Iron Bridge Gorge Museum Trust

Brunel's Paddington Station was inspired by Paxton's design for the Great Exhibition's Crystal Palace   © University of Bristol

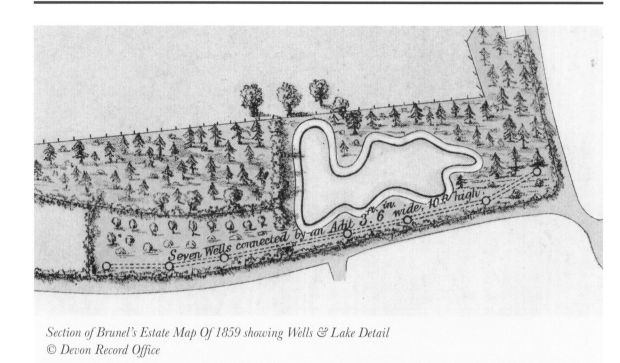

Section of Brunel's Estate Map Of 1859 showing Wells & Lake Detail
© Devon Record Office

descend – the engine forcing the water into the reservoir [at the top of the hill] for use in the mansion when built and also for the use of the gardeners. The explosion took place about every 20 seconds and was very violent and could be heard for a mile away.'

Brunel was fortunate to have this ready access to water, due to the proximity of the Watcombe clay beds, which later provided the raw material for the famous Watcombe pottery. Water supply presented a serious problem in Torquay. Quite close to Watcombe, at the Havelock Brewery, the drill passed through 20 feet of red and blue marl and then 350 feet of limestone without finding water. For many years the water supply in Torquay was turned on for only a few hours each day, and additional supplies were brought in from Dartmoor by 1858. (Brunel's son, Henry, later became involved from time to time with what he termed 'the beastly Torquay waterworks,' and in 1877 was appointed Torquay's water engineer.)

William Henry Grant who had worked for Brunel as he started to create his Watcombe estate. Grant was twelve when Brunel came to Watcombe, twenty-three when Brunel died. His memoirs describe details of work carried out. He also wrote about mechanics of the gas powered water pumping system. © Devon Record Office
Image: Rick Hillard

Brunel's second son, Henry, became involved from time to time with Torquay waterworks,' and in 1877 was appointed Torquay's water engineer

Shelter-belts – and the Concept of the Great Eastern

Before turning to Brunel's planting of trees, it is worth stressing that as an engineer he had unrivalled experience of the properties and uses of timber. Some of his earliest memories would have been of his father's timber handling machinery at Chatham, and of the family timber-yard at Battersea. Later he used timber effectively for the roof of his great train shed at Temple Meads, and for the lofty viaducts in Devon and Cornwall. But his most dramatic and effective use of timber was in saving the stranded *Great Britain* from destruction. When he arrived at the scene of the disaster, late in 1846, he realised at once that what had been attempted so far was inadequate, and that unless drastic action was taken it would soon be too late. Whole trees must be used to form a protective palisade: massive trunks were to be lashed together to withstand the worst of the winter storms. Pine was used at first, but proved too inflexible, splintering under the changing pressures of the waves. Then beech was substituted, felled from the estates of the nearest landowners. To those beech trees, flexing responsively to the waves, we owe the presence of *Great Britain* at Bristol today. A contemporary painting shows at least fifty great tree-trunks already incorporated in the protective shield. Another is being hoisted into position and yet another is being trundled across the sand, perched precariously on a flat-topped cart.

In December 1846 Brunel was sacrificing beech trees to save his ship. One year later – almost as if in reparation – he was advertising for a man with 'great knowledge of tree cultivation' to plant whole shelter-belts of beeches.

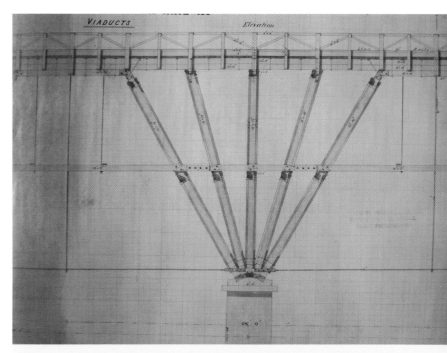

Brunel used timber effectively for the lofty viaducts in Devon and Cornwall. This design was used in several different locations. © *Network Rail*

Brunel's most dramatic and effective use of timber was in saving the stranded Great Britain from destruction in 1846 © Science & Society

Brunel's correspondence concerned the planting of shelter-belts to protect the house, gardens and more tender trees from the savage winds that batter Devonshire in autumn and winter. (Unfortunately several of these shelter-belt trees were felled by developers building bungalows on parts of the Watcombe estate. As a result the severe storm which struck Devon on 25th January 1990 felled hundreds of Brunel's trees.)
Lowdes Patemen Collection

The earliest mention of trees in Brunel's correspondence concerned the planting of shelter-belts to protect the house, gardens and more tender trees from the savage winds that batter Devonshire in autumn and winter. (Unfortunately several of these shelter-belt trees were felled by developers building bungalows on parts of the Watcombe estate. As a

result the severe storm which struck Devon on 25th January 1990 felled hundreds of Brunel's trees.) In November 1851 there was discussion with Dawson on whether to pay £200 to Mr. Blackaller so that the estate could be extended northwards to provide shelter from north-westerly gales. It seems that local landowners were now cashing in on Brunel's known desire to extend his holdings. He grumbled that £150 would be well-paid for the two acres of indifferent land, but left it to Dawson's discretion to go up to £200 if he thought that the purchase would result in an improvement to the existing grounds. Through his railway activities Brunel was well accustomed to making 'take it or leave it' offers. In this instance it was to be made quite clear to Blackaller that the offer was final: a belt of trees would be planted along that northern boundary, and once this had been done no further land would be wanted.

The years 1852 and 1853 passed by, and there are very few recorded letters concerning Watcombe. This was possibly due in part to preoccupations elsewhere – floating the great tube of the Chepstow Bridge, completing the design for the Saltash Bridge and starting work on the Cornwall Railway. But above all this was the period when Brunel began to plan and design the ship that was to become *Great Eastern*. To a great extent the construction of railways and associated bridges was a challenge that had been met: the coming task was to meet the challenge of effective and economical ocean transport. Towards the end of 1851 Brunel seems to have set out the essential principles of a ship that would be double-skinned, propelled by both paddlewheels and screw, and containing enough fuel to complete long-distance voyages without re-coaling. By 25th March 1852 came the appearance in Brunel's sketch book of the monster ship described so dramatically in Rolt's biography: '…the eye is suddenly arrested by a sketch of an extraordinary steamship as long as the page is wide and bristling with funnels and masts. The drawing is headed "East India Steamship" and beneath it is scribbled casually the note: "Say 600 ft x 65 ft x 30 ft", dimensions which any contemporary shipwright would have regarded with absolute incredulity.' Getting this ship accepted, financed, constructed and launched would occupy much of the remainder of Brunel's life.

According to Rolt's interpretation the *Great Eastern* became to Brunel '…all consuming, and the dream of a peaceful retirement to the West Country was driven ever further into the background of his thoughts.' But the paucity of letters about Watcombe is far from conclusive. Any property purchase generates a period of intense activity, followed by a period of comparative calm. (Smaller land purchases did in fact continue, Brunel writing to Dawson about this on 14th April 1854 and 24th May 1856.) Grant's memoirs record that most of the initial work on the estate had been completed by 1851 and many of the

staff had been paid off. Forsyth had now been in post for three years and knew what needed to be done: most estate-management decisions would now be taken during Brunel's visits and would not be recorded in letters. There is an interesting example of this in a letter to Dawson on 2nd March, 1853: 'I will of course build the wall as proposed by Mr. Wall which is only reasonable – but in setting out the line of the wall I propose to take a give and take line…I expect to be down on Saturday and will set out exactly what I want.' (In his estate planning as in his engineering Brunel was a man determined to have things just the way he wanted them.) There is a further example in a letter to Dawson on 1st November 1851. He included a rough sketch of how he wanted some groups of trees planted, provided he was within his legal rights in setting them out in this fashion. '…I should not like to begin by committing myself to an illegal act. If my right is limited to a belt I shall only plant a belt – and then half my advantage is lost.'

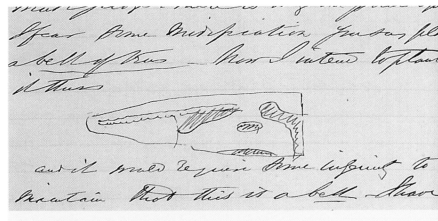

Brunel was a man determined to have things just the way he wanted them. In this letter to Dawson on 1st November 1851, he included a rough sketch of how he wanted some groups of trees planted, provided he was within his legal rights in setting them out in this fashion.
© *University of Bristol*

Brunel's Watcombe Garden Book

The relatively few letters on Watcombe confirm that further land was still being purchased – firm evidence that Brunel's Watcombe Adventure was far from being a lost cause. Most powerful evidence of all is a flimsy notebook with marbled covers, written up in Brunel's own angular scrawl. Rolt saw this notebook – and made limited use of it – when surveying family documents at 'Walwick Hall', the house of Sir Humphrey Noble in Northumberland. After being 'missing' for many years it has recently surfaced, and is now safely held with other Brunel records at Bristol University. (Catalogued as follows: DM 1954/1/1: Watcombe Garden Book. Notebook by Isambard Kingdom Brunel describing his garden at Watcombe, overlooking Babbacombe Bay, near Torquay,Devon…32 pages (including one loose sheet), stiff marbled covers.) This flimsy volume proves beyond all doubt that Watcombe had not become a lost cause in the later 1850's; that much of the surviving landscape was developed during those years; and that Watcombe was as important a facet of Brunel's extraordinary genius as any of his major works of engineering.

This has been recognised at the conclusion of Dan Cruickshank's excellent Introduction to Steven Brindle's *Brunel, the Man who Built the World*: 'This beautiful landscape, with its subtle and creative manipulation of nature, is a perfect complement to Brunel's nearby iron and powerfully functional Saltash Bridge. Together they reveal the nature of the man – the incredible span of his genius and his achievements.' Two pages of the Watcombe Garden Book are given over to drawings of trees – for instance 'Araucaria in Sea Walk, Aug. 15, 1853,'and a bushier 'Araucaria in round clump of Lower Garden, Aug 31, 1853.' The sketches reveal a delight in the way in which nature, not man, is taking charge of events and imposing its own pattern. For Brunel this must have been a welcome and refreshing change. Most of his work was involved with structures that must be rigid, firm, unmoveable – other than a small settlement in a bridge or the necessary slight 'give' in a railway track. Things that moved were the enemy to be countered - the river that broke into the Thames Tunnel, or the waves that threatened the *Great Britain* with destruction. But now it is Nature that is in charge - and it is to her tune that man must dance.

A close study of Brunel's proceedings at Watcombe provides a balance to many interpretations of his personality. The Brunel's family motto – derived from holding the posting contract at Hacqueville – was 'En Avant', along with the symbol of a spur. He always drove his own staff and his contractors hard, calling frequently for 'more speed!' (Angus Buchanan terms him 'a driven man.') But if he was a slave-driver with others he was also creating a treadmill for himself, as he confessed to John Horsley in August 1848 when depressed by the collapse of so many railway schemes. 'You and many others may think of my life as a pleasant one because I am of a happy disposition but from morning to night, from one end of the year to the other, it is the life of a slave. I am never my own master and I always have an overwhelming quantity of work which must be done by certain days.' Adrian Vaughan in his study, *Brunel, Engineering Knight-Errant*, provides plentiful evidence of how much of this over-work was due to faulty or unrealistic planning, or by Brunel's insistence on supervising every facet of the work. Much of his 'bossiness' was probably due to the innate insecurity that emerged in his private journals; but part of the explanation lies in that plaintive phrase – 'I am never my own master.' Always there was a Board of Directors to be placated: shareholders' meetings to be assured of future profits.

The Brunel's family motto – derived from holding the posting contract at Hacqueville – was 'En Avant', along with the symbol of a spur.

At Watcombe, alone, Brunel could be his own master, work at his own pace – or rather at nature's pace. Here the watchword was no longer 'En Avant' but 'Festina Lente' – the punning motto of the Onslow family, 'Make Haste Slowly.' Here was a man reputed to be always in a hurry: yet it was some time before he embarked on his major tree-planting; ten years before he began to build his house. These were years of careful preparation, of contact with experts, of gradual improvement of the land with those cart-loads of peat. (Brunel was certainly a follower of the old adage: 'a shilling for the plant and a pound for the planting.') Under Watcombe's influence Brunel seemed to become a gentler, kindlier man. Here he could be the good companion that others encountered only when he was not driven by the needs of the job: the kind of man described by George Clark the ironmaster. 'His light and joyous disposition was very attractive. At no time was he stern, but when travelling or off work he was like a boy set free. There was no fun for which he was not ready.' In the year 1858, just as Brunel's life was ending, the poet Dorothy Gurney was born. Her words, somewhat hackneyed now, are writ large in every Garden Centre:

'The kiss of the sun for pardon
The song of the birds for mirth,
One is nearer God's Heart in a garden
Than anywhere else on earth.'

Even when words become hackneyed they may still bear truth: for it was at Watcombe that John Horsley rejoiced to hear Brunel speaking of the efficacy of prayer.

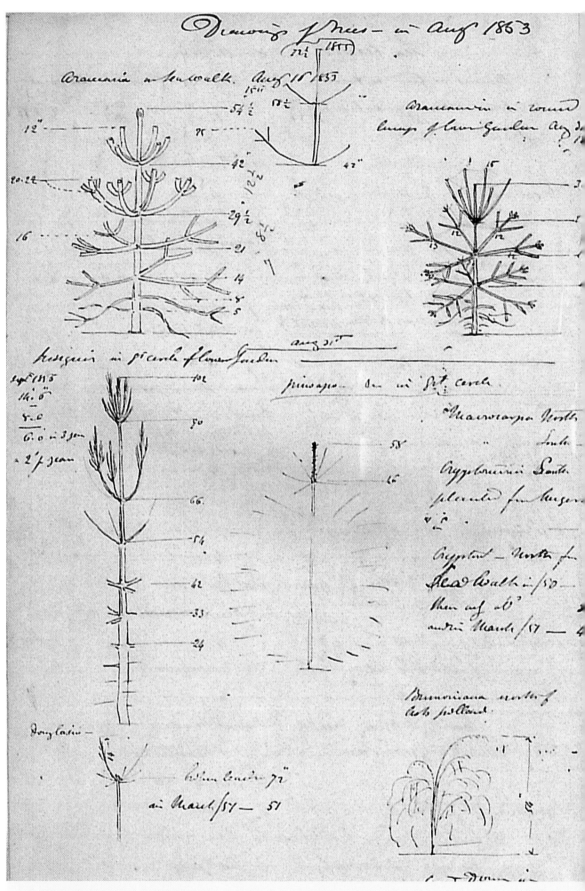

Two pages of the Watcombe Garden Book are given over to drawings of trees – for instance 'Araucaria in Sea Walk, Aug. 15, 1853,' and a bushier 'Araucaria in round clump of Lower Garden, Aug 31, 1853.' The sketches reveal a delight in the way in which nature, not man, is taking charge of events and imposing its own pattern.
© *University of Bristol*

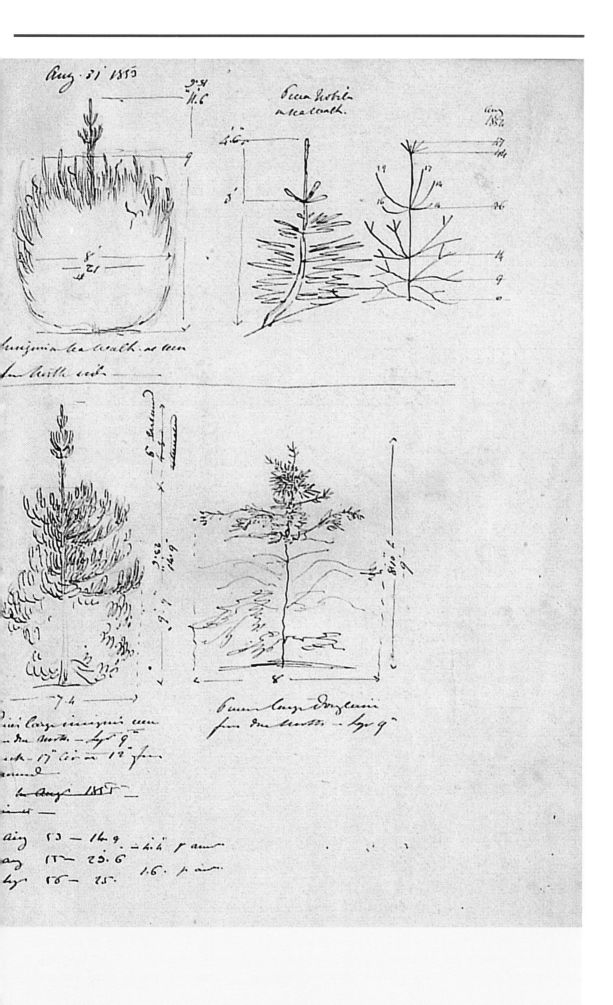

Brunel's attitude to people when he was down at Watcombe appears to have been different. Even when he crossed swords with a man like Daniel Woodley his approach, though firm, was dignified and correct. There was none of that acerbic, sarcastic – sometimes downright rude – language that he used with his assistants, contractors and competitors. His relations with his local employees seem to have been friendly, and his treatment of them generous. It was exceptional in those days for workers to be given any form of paid holiday, but this is what Brunel did in September 1851, as described by the Torquay newspaper. He was heavily involved with the Great Exhibition, and decided that all his estate workers should have a five day holiday in London so that they could view it. 'They occupied the bodies of two carriages and started in high spirits. They were met by a guide at the Paddington terminus and conducted to the Crystal Palace, the British Museum, the Thames Tunnel, and other Lions of London…the whole of their expenses were defrayed by their kind employer, and their weekly wages paid as if they had continued their work.' Some allowance should perhaps be made for *De mortuis nil nisi bonum*, but on his death a local memorial fund was established, distinct from the national appeal: the local paper commented: 'doubtless many of the humbler classes, who have experienced Mr. Brunel's generosity, will be glad to give their mite…' It was the tragedy of Brunel's Watcombe Adventure that this was the

one area of his life where he took his time: and it was here that time overtook him, with his house unbuilt and his estate unfinished.

Brunel's Garden Book shows that some specimen trees (subsequently measured at various dates up to 1856) were planted as early as 1849. There may have been an earlier notebook, now vanished; but the surviving book begins – quite neatly set out – on August 15th 1853. It is headed: 'Water Arrangements – As to areas to be watered'. A list follows of five different garden areas totalling just over 50 acres – just over a third of the eventual estate. Brunel estimated the cubic ft. of water that would be required in a dry summer: 'This will therefore require 24 days pumping of 10,000 cubic ft. per day which is about the practical limit of that engine, leaving an hour or two per day to supply lower grounds.' The three following pages contain entries made between 15th and 19th August with further thoughts about the water supply – especially how much would be needed making allowance for evaporation. The main reservoir on the ridge would be circular with a diameter of 71' 6" and a depth of 10' – holding about 40,000 cubic ft.: two smaller reservoirs would hold 10,000 cubic ft. between them, the whole requiring about five days pumping. Brunel then moved on to consider the requirements for a planned fountain playing for 12 hours a day: surplus water from the fountain basin would flow down the hillside to water the lower grounds. Total length of

Water arrangements

As to areas to be watered

The space included within the carriage drive
& back road to the North the S O R^d and steps to
the East — the wood walk and quarry to
W 1.   the West and cross lane to the lister say   12 acres.

The west Hill — including all west of above up
W 2.   to Poultry yard —   about —   18.

Sea walk ground being all east of S O Road
W 3.   to the upper hedge —   5½

W 4 —   Watcombe avenues &c   2.

W 5 —   Lower Grounds   16.

Say that in a dry month W 1 may
require an average of 2" which on I give
4" over the beds assuming them at 3 acres
and 1⅓ over grass of 9 acres —
on require —   3 acres × — 12 × 2   24.
W 2 say — that over 14 acres of grass — 1"   14.
and 4 acres of plantation &c o 3 —   12.
W 3 — half at 1" and half o 3   11
W 4 — say 2" —   4.
                                              ――
                                              65

43560 × 65 ÷ 12 =   236000 — cube ft —
This w^d therefore require 24 days pumping of 10.000
ft p day which is about the practical limit
of the engine — leaving an hour or two p day to supply
lower grounds ――

*Brunel's Watcombe Garden Book commences with entries made on August 15th 1853 about water arrangements
for the estate. This is followed by details of engine arrangements.   © University of Bristol*

Engine arrangements

Finally determined to carry the main by rockery thence either by lane or grass to east side of ground pond up in direction of new path to a point opposite the ... gate at about the level of 460. at this point to branch to the summit reservoir

on Brereton Hill — and up to house — thence back road round to the wood hill clump — at the fork — to have a stop return valve and a bypass to let the upper pressure back either main if desired

After passing the line to supply fountain the waste water from whence to run into a reservoir below the basin and thence supply a main descending to Elms and branching into first main at fork and round to araucaria bed & west —

[margin note:] Aug 18 1851 / ... / ... Hannan...

Levels of the various dead water

Mean level in engine well — say —	275	0
Lower reservoir & pond	295	20
Rockery ponds — about —	360	85
... reception to command whole		
of flower gardens —	430	115
Fountain — reservoir — mean level —	483	208
wood hill — do — mean level —	540	
top water	545	260
House tank — bottom —	540	
top water	545	265
Main reservoir — mean —	550	
top water	555	270
Standings to do —	570	295

Details of engine arrangements.   © University of Bristol

the main would be about 1200 yards, together with 400 yards of secondary pipe. Stop-return valves and by-passes would be provided, along with about 10 cocks for attaching hoses.

Brunel was back to the front page on 18th August to plan the laying of the pipe-work up the valley to the reservoirs, and to the various locations – such as the Araucaria bed – where water would be required. A neat table set out the heights of the various locations, from 275 ft at the Engine well to 570 ft. at the laundry: water would thus need to be pumped a maximum vertical height of 295 ft.

A whole year later, on 19th August 1854, Brunel was again at work on page 4, completing his plans by estimating the needs of the rockery – probably a gallon a minute. Different options for providing this without wastage were discussed – 'perhaps the best way would be to have two pipes from the tank.' Negotiations with neighbouring landowners must have been taking place, and there was now a new proposal for the main reservoir. 'I think I shall make the main reservoir (now settled to be on Hammond's Hill) 100' diameter (probably octagon) and 10 ft deep, thus to hold 78,540 cub. ft. or about a week's pumping.'

CHAPTER 4:
The Brunel/Forsyth Partnership

Trees – and still more Trees

In 1853 Brunel was back at Watcombe in October, with leisure enough to push ahead with his tree-planting plans. He recorded on October 23rd that there seemed every probability of getting Hammond's ground, (where the main reservoir was to be sited), and this provided the opportunity for planting a good background for the house. For the first time he demonstrates that this was a joint family project: Mary had suggested that a dense clump of Insignis (Monterey Pine) would look very fine; 'if they withstand the wind nothing could be better.' Calculations follow, working out

This clump of Monterey Pine (Cupressus Macrocarpa) in the grounds of Brunel Manor may well be that which Mary Brunel suggested should be planted. Image: Tracey Elliot-Reep

the spacing of trees in the various clumps, leading to a neat table listing the trees required: 450 Insignis, 800 Austrian, 800 Scotch Fir, and 700 Larch. To shelter the young trees from the wind would require hurdles: the quantity of these was also calculated.

1854 must have seen Brunel frequently in Devon. In May the Great Cylinder to form the central pier of the Saltash Bridge was floated, so this was a crucial

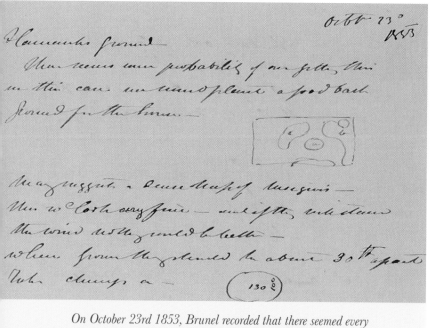

On October 23rd 1853, Brunel recorded that there seemed every probability of getting Hammond's ground, (where the main reservoir was to be sited), and this provided the opportunity for planting a good background for the house. © University of Bristol

Mary and Florence Brunel. Anonymous

time for the success of the project. But on 16th July, with the cylinder successfully in place, Brunel was able to relax and turn his mind to his trees once more. Having provided for shelter-belts, and for the background to his future house, he could now consider the more distant vistas. (The creation of vistas – as at Kew – was of course Nesfield's important contribution to landscaping.) Brunel was fortunate in his time, for this was the great age for tree-planting: plant-hunters were scouring the world and risking their lives in the search for new species; specialist nurserymen were propagating and supplying young stock.

Tree planting on a grand scale had started in Scotland a century earlier, with the Dickson family's tree nursery supplying both Scotland and the North of England. There it was that young John Veitch learned his trade before coming down from Scotland to seek his fortune. It was this 'flying start' in Scotland that gave so many young Scotsmen a competitive advantage when it came to finding a good position in England. (There was considerable resentment: one English garden designer complained that 'by the help of a little Learning, and a great deal of Impudence, they invade the Southern Province.') John Veitch may have had both learning and impudence, he certainly had business acumen. He laid out the landscaped park at 'Killerton' for the Aclands in the 1770's, progressed to become Agent there, and greatly extended the parkland for the 'Great Sir Thomas Acland' in the early 1800's. There was now a much more elaborate concept at 'Killerton': there would be grass glades, gravel walks, thickets and 'single Trees …to Forrest parts of the Lawn for your amusement for years to come.' Graham Stuart Thomas considered that 'Killerton' 'gives perhaps the most impressive skyline of any arboretum in the country.'

In May 1854 the Great Cylinder to form the central pier of the Saltash Bridge was floated, so this was a crucial time for the success of the project. But on 16th July, with the cylinder successfully in place, Brunel was able to relax and turn his mind to his trees once more.
© Public Records Picture Library

John Veitch founded a dynasty of nurserymen, and the great Pinetum at 'Bicton' was planted by a later Veitch generation for the Rolle family in 1838. So great was the demand for trees that the Veitch family developed an extensive Tree Nursery in the St. David's area of Exeter. Landowners vied with each other to secure the latest and finest specimens, and Brunel was not likely to be backward in such a competition. One example is

This Monkey Puzzle (Araucaria Araucana) tree in the lower grounds (Brunel Woods) today may well be this same tree fully matured.
Image: Tracey Elliot-Reep

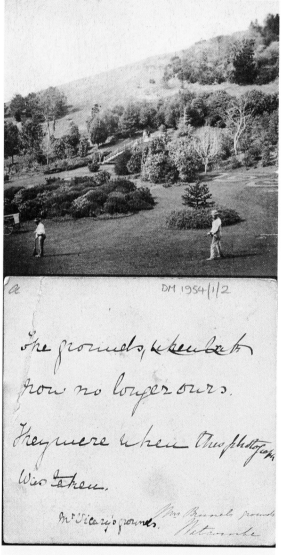

This Brunel family photograph shows people walking and working in the lower grounds. Note the small Monkey Puzzle (Araucaria Araucana) tree and compare this with Brunel's drawing on page 50
© University of Bristol

the Monkey Puzzle, (araucaria araucana), considered so important that Brunel specified arrangements for watering them. These had been first introduced to Britain by the plant hunter Archibald Menzies around 1795. He secured them by the simple expedient of pocketing some seeds from the dessert table of the Governor of Chile, where they were considered a delicacy. (They are, in fact, extremely palatable.) The Monkey Puzzle was reintroduced in the 1840's, probably by Veitch's agent, William Lobb., and the great avenue at Bicton in Devon was planted around the year 1843. (This was the year when Veitch first

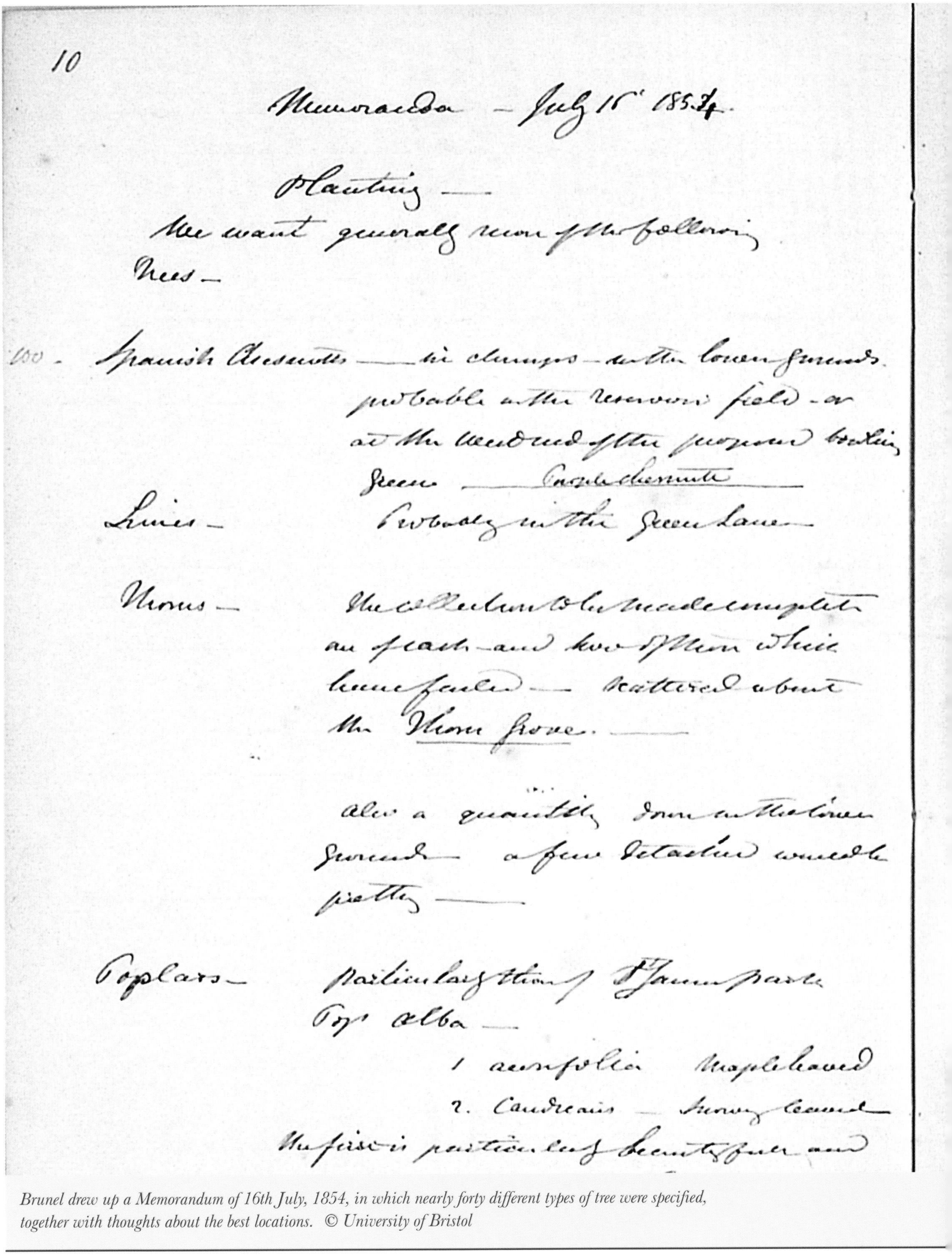

10

Memoranda – July 16ᵗʰ 1854.

Planting –

We want generally more of the following
trees –

100 . Spanish Chestnuts — in clumps - in the lower grounds.
probable in the reservoir field - or
at the lend end of the proposed broad
green — Castle chestnut

Limes – probably in the Green Lane

Thorns – the collection to be made complete
as of each and two of them which
have failed — scattered about
the Thorn grove. —

also a quantity down in the lower
grounds a few detached would be
pretty —

Poplars – particularly those of fauns park
Pop. alba —

1 aurifolia Maple leaved
2 Candicans — honey leaved
the first is particularly beautiful and

---

*Brunel drew up a Memorandum of 16th July, 1854, in which nearly forty different types of tree were specified,
together with thoughts about the best locations. © University of Bristol*

View towards Portland from the Sea Walk
Image: Tracey Elliot-Reep

advertised these trees in the *Gardeners' Chronicle*, 'having raised many thousands from seed.') Brunel was planting them in some quantity a few years later when they were still a sensation. Other recent introductions included Deodar (1831): Monterey Pine (1833): Austrian Pine (1835): Monterey Cypress (1838): Atlas Cedar (1840): Western Red Cedar (1853). These were the kind of tree that caught Brunel's imagination and which he was determined to include in his planting.

He drew up a Memorandum of 16th July, 1854, in which nearly forty different types of tree were specified, together with thoughts about the best locations. There would be Spanish Chestnuts in clumps in the lower ground, in the reservoir field, and at the end of the proposed bowling green. Limes would look good along the Green Lane at the foot of the valley, and Poplars in front of the pond. He specially noted some forms

of Poplar that he had seen in St. James Park – possibly Nesfield had walked there with him and pointed them out. Brunel had certainly kept his eyes open and had seen 'some beautiful purple-leaved Hazels' – also in St. James Park. Four types of Gleditsias, (Honey Locusts) were specified, along with Maples ('some of the prettiest') and Tulip Trees for the Lower Ground and Green Lane. Over 20 types of Pine were to be planted on the Lower Ground, five types of Ash, Luccombe Oak, Silver Fir and Elders – 'I must try some on the dry hill.' To complete his planting he intended to draw up a list of suitable Underwoods: he proposed such plants as St. John's Wort, Periwinkle, Berberis, Rhododendrons and Ivy. To supplement the Underwoods there would be a wide range of Valley Shrubs, listed on page 13 of the notebook. Eleven different types were specified, including Rhus, Acacia, Spirea, Buddleia and Pittosporum. There followed a reminder to 'sow plenty of creepers for feathering off beds.' – the function of these creepers was to ensure that the new beds merged into the landscape. Some of the fourteen creepers featured among the Underwoods already listed: among the others were Escalonia, Honeysuckle, Sempervivums, Thyme, Small Heaths, and Creeping Evergreen Thorn.

A month later, on 19th August, Brunel set out his **Memorandum for this year's planting**. He was now considering the placing of a few trees here and there for the required effect: Acacias in Rocky

Lane; some Poplars by the pond; a group of Horse Chestnut and Birch at the NW corner of Lower Ground; more Willow 'at back of pond and in some one conspicuous place in front.' Here he was planting for foliage contrast, as noted later by that reporter for the *Gardeners' Chronicle*, who attributed the successful planting to 'a man who knew what he was about.' Two days later, on 21st August, Brunel continued his survey of different parts of the estate. To screen the turnpike road there were to be some dark trees to break the line – Yews, Turkey Oaks and Atlas Cedars. In the Lower Garden he would bring in some Arbutus, Berberis, Hollies and double gorse clumps. He was now planning the more distant parts of his wood walk: 'get what will grow there.'

Next he turned his attention to Sea Walk Hill. This was part of the spectacular drive he would create on the far side of the Teignmouth Turnpike. Avenues would be planted, affording occasional dramatic glimpses of the sea. First there would be views to distant Portland; then an exciting stretch along the summit of Giant Rock; finally the splendid view across Torbay to Berry Head. Scotch Firs and Yews were to be planted thickly, along with a few Atlas Cedars, while Hollies were to be transplanted to form hedges: (it was later noted that this was 'done Dec. 54.') Further up the hill there were to be Mountain Pine 'on upper and lower edge of sea walk and all over the barren slope of hill – and try some Austrians [pines]

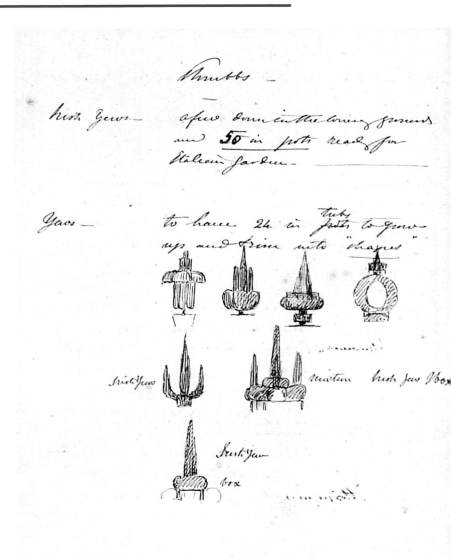

Brunel's sketches of topiary designs   © *University of Bristol*

On page 18 of Brunel's Garden book, comes the heading – Italian Garden. There would be untrimmed yew intermixed with junipers, Cotoneaster creeping down the slope, and a background of Cedars and Deodars. © *University of Bristol*

The plan of the Italian Garden with the fountain detail was drawn in one of Brunel's sketch books.
© *University of Bristol*

among them. Get rid of furrows. Transplant yews, now along edge of Scotch firs.' On the exposed seaward stretch there would be an 'Upper Sea Walk' lined with Mountain Pine and Austrian Pine, both trees that are widely planted to withstand gales from the sea.

It was in this 1854 Memorandum that, for the first time, there appears some indication of plans for the formal gardens around the house. Lavish use would be made of Irish Yew, which had become widely available from around 1820 and was much in demand for topiary: 'A few down in the Lower Grounds, and 50 in pots for the Italian Garden.' There would also be Common Yew: 'to have 24 in tubs to grow up and train into "shapes".' (Below this item Brunel has sketched seven of these intended "shapes".) Finally, on page 18, comes the heading – **Italian Garden**. There would be untrimmed yew intermixed with junipers, Cotoneaster creeping down the slope, and a background of Cedars and Deodars. This Italian Garden would form an important element of the finished design: during his trips to Italy Brunel seems to have collected statues, urns and other items to be displayed there.

'...Great knowledge of tree cultivation...'

This, it will be remembered, is what Brunel sought when he made his first enquiries into the capabilities of Alexander Forsyth. Forsyth certainly had

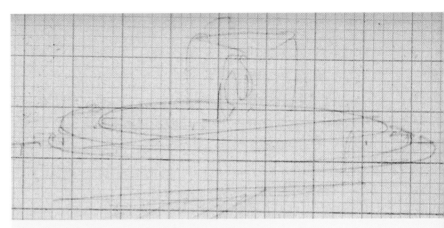

Fountain section of Itralian Garden drawing.
© University of Bristol

The Italian Garden (as a tennis court in 1930s) is surrounded by many of Brunel's original trees as listed in his planting notes
Image: Brunel Manor

Section of estate map of 1859 showing tank for fountain in Italian Garden © Devon Record Office

plenty of experience, first at 'Alderley Park' in Cheshire, and then in creating the Arboretum for the Earl of Shrewsbury at 'Alton Towers'. He had arrived there in 1839, following a recommendation from Augustus Pugin, who was then at work converting the house and grounds into 'a Gothic Wonderland' – (the sub-title of Michael Fisher's book on Alton Towers.) Pugin noted in his letter that Forsyth was strongly recommended by Joseph Knight, the well-known horticulturist who ran a successful nursery garden in the King's Road, Chelsea. Pugin underlined Knight's name and also the words 'strongly recommended', adding that he had 'no doubt that he [Forsyth] will answer the lord's expectations in every respect.' To some extent Forsyth seems to have been called in to repair earlier mistakes. When Loudon visited 'Alton Towers' in 1831 he had criticised the lavish use of temples and ornaments: it was all 'too much' and in 'excessively bad taste.' The famous designer had been called on for advice – nearly all of which had been ignored. This no doubt explains the acerbity of his comments in his *An Encyclopaedie of Gardening* in 1834: '…a lofty prospect tower, not built on the highest part of the ground; bridges without water underneath;ponds and lakes on the top of hills…' A considerable amount of tree-planting was required to provide setting and background for all this architecture: Forsyth was given the job and must have been kept busy.

And not just on tree-planting, for Pugin was busy stage-managing spectacular events, 'sometimes in collaboration with Alexander Forsyth.' Another example of Forsyth's involvement was when the earl's recently-wedded daughter arrived with her husband, Prince Doria Pamphili, to be greeted by an assembly of a hundred tenants, the Alton Band, boys and girls of Alton School with baskets of flowers and bouquets. The cavalcade wound its way beneath a triumphant floral arch, 'the tastefulness and beauty of which reflects great credit on Mr. Forsyth, his lordship's head gardener.' The demands imposed by the earl's lavish entertaining may well have palled after a time. Whenever there was entertaining, the Armoury and Galleries were banked high with flowers and plants to be admired by the guests; but the gardeners had to be on duty in the early hours to tidy up the place as soon as the last carriage had departed: the earl insisted that not a trace must be left by breakfast time.

So Forsyth may well have been attracted by a post in Devon which offered tree-cultivation rather than 'fancy gardening'. On the other hand, his obituary in the *Manchester Evening News* stressed that the condition of things was 'far from romantic' during the early years at Watcombe. The article hints that there were brushes with Mr Cogswell and his gangs of railway navvies, whose activities must have clashed at times

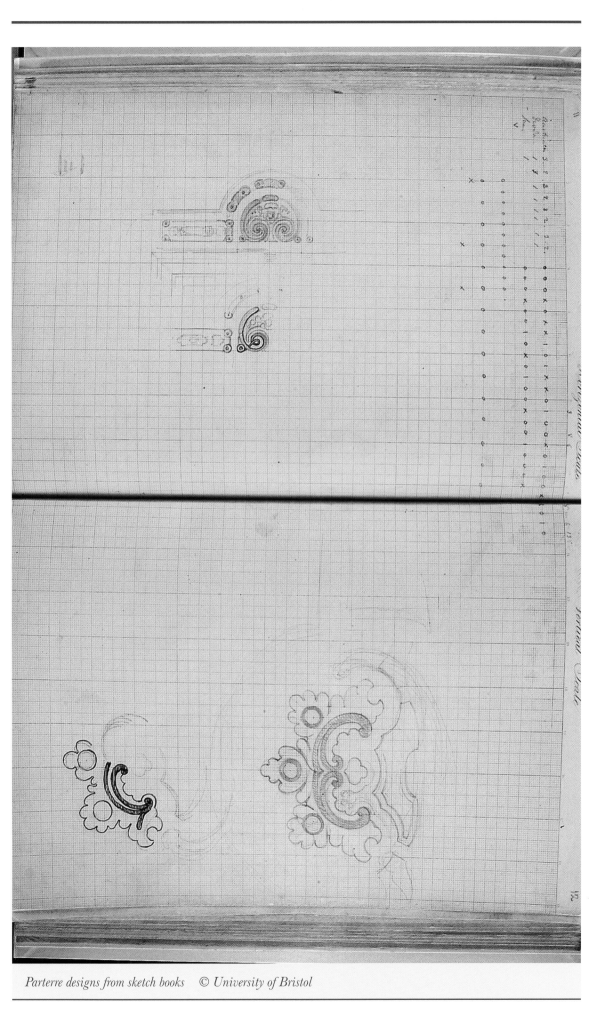

Parterre designs from sketch books   © *University of Bristol*

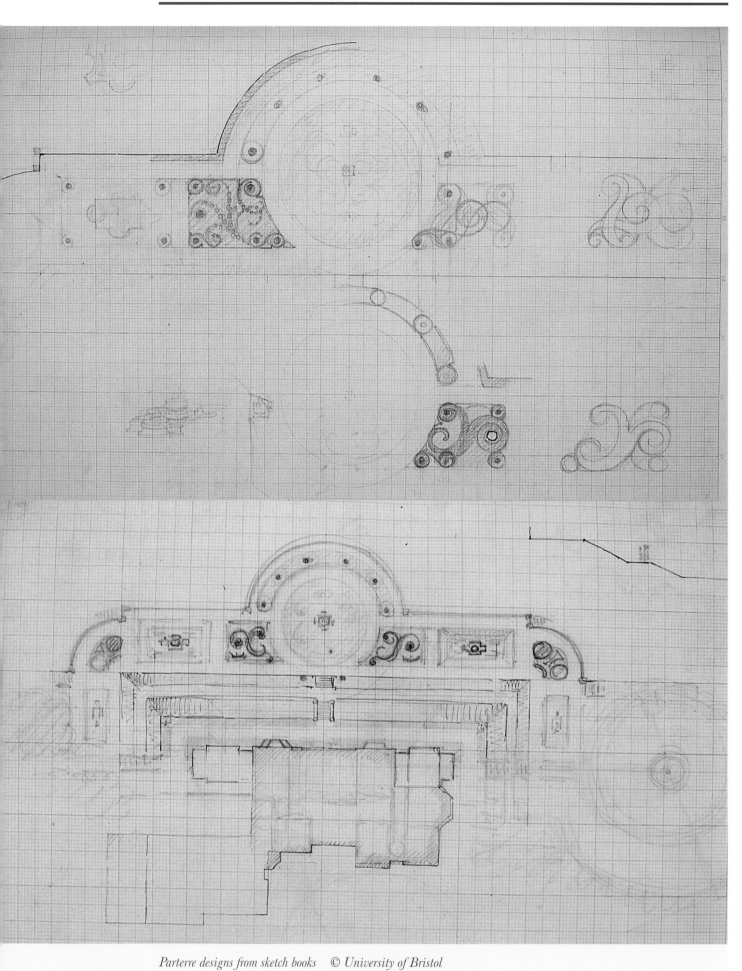

Parterre designs from sketch books   © *University of Bristol*

Top: Parterre designs from sketch books © *University of Bristol   Above Image: Tracey Elliot-Reep*

with Forsyth's gentler pursuits. Small wonder that he had recourse to his favourite Hollyleaf tea as a soothing drink, and enjoyed his meals of Rhubarb flowers; 'the pouches of unopened flowers bearing the same relation to the leaves of Rhubarb that Cauliflowers do to Cabbage leaves.' Certainly he was a man of enquiring mind. In 1856, for example, he was writing to the *Mark Lane Express*, (reprinted in the *Torquay Directory*), about 'Native Guano in Torbay'. He had discovered at low tide 'a seam or vein of compressed vegetable matter, friable and easily reduced to powder, after the fashion of leaf mould...I have for years past had some of it carted for manure...It is the deposit of centuries accumulated in this creek or bay from storms, being pure sea-weed, black as ink...'

In general Forsyth was noted for his genial nature, which 'gained him the favour of many of the local gentry,' but he clashed with local hunting parties – 'their frequent raids upon the beautiful estate under his care were sore trials to him.' On at least one occasion he sent a man with a hare's skin to lay a false trail away from the estate in the direction of Stoke-in-Teignhead.

Brunel, then, had an experienced man at his elbow when he set out his planting programme. There is no indication

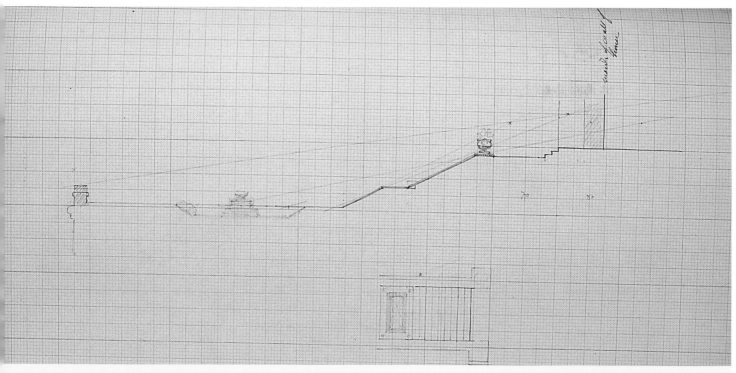

Terrace plans, cross section, showing lines of vision from the lounge towards the view © University of Bristol

The terrace 1960s shows these plans were followed   Image: Brunel Manor

anywhere in the Garden Book that 'Mr Forsyth advises' or that 'Mr Forsyth suggests': but he would probably have been at Brunel's shoulder – or at least in the background – to give his advice. At various places in the notebook there are deletions and insertions that may well have been due to some prompting from Forsyth along the lines of: 'Haven't you forgotten…?' or 'Would it perhaps be a good idea to do so and so?' Another source of advice was almost certainly the 'Mr. Nesfield of Eton College' to whom Brunel applied to seek a reference for Forsyth. Clearly Brunel knew him only by reputation, ('is he the landscape gardener?'), but this opening seems to have led to further contact with a man who was one of the foremost tree experts in the country. Nesfield seems to have strayed into landscape design almost by accident, for his early career consisted in fighting with Wellington's army in Spain. He then took up landscape painting in water-colour and won a reputation for portrayal of both still and moving water. Around 1836 Nesfield designed a garden for Salvin, his brother-in-law, which led to a new career as landscape designer at the age of forty-three. Rise to prominence was rapid, and it was in 1844 that he took over at Kew and began setting out the great vistas and avenues which provide his 'indelible signature on today's Kew.'

Nesfield was also prominent in the redesigning of London's Royal Parks, especially St. James Park and Regent's Park. (That his work is still cherished today was shown during a House of Lords Debate in October 2000. Lord St. John of Fawsley urged the Government to get rid of some statues and sculptures 'which are disfiguring and have disfigured for over 12 months the Nesfield Garden.') Nesfield's feeling for water in all its forms led to the fantastic fountains at Witley Court, work at Castle Howard, and commissions at around 260 estates. Whether he had any direct influence on the design of Watcombe Park is uncertain: apart from seeking a reference for Forsyth there is no other record in Brunel's correspondence. Very little of Nesfield's work was done in the West Country and he was very busy at the time with grand projects in London and elsewhere. Probably his influence was restricted to giving some general advice on layout, and possibly demonstrating this during walks in the London parks. (Down in Devon Brunel could have seen many examples of landscape design such as those tree planting schemes by the Veitch family at 'Killerton', and 'Bicton'. Closer to hand near Newton Abbot were the landscaped grounds of the Templer family at 'Stover' and 'Sandford Orleigh' – soon to be retirement home for Baker of the Nile. There is plentiful testimony to Brunel's ability to master new skills and new techniques. His Garden Book provides proof that he was no fumbling beginner.)

CHAPTER 5:
Brunel's Local Involvements

The good Employer

Brunel's Garden Book is perhaps the strongest evidence that his work at Watcombe was something in which he could take a powerful – even passionate – personal interest. In no sense would he be an absentee landowner with little interest in local affairs. At an early stage Mrs Brunel founded a local school, probably in one of the roomier cottages in the local village of Barton. It was certainly well-established by 7th September 1853 when the children were given a day to remember, as described in a local paper.

'Mrs Brunel gave tea and supper to the workmen employed on the estate at Barton, and their families. The children from the school at Barton which their truly generous lady has established for the education of the infants of the poor, seventy of which were first treated with a sight of the beautiful pleasure grounds, and after partaking of various amusements provided for their entertainment were regaled with tea, tarts, buns etc. The workmen and their families, great and small, came on the ground at half-past two and after various games of football, racing, jumping etc, sat down to tea in a large rustic house, neatly fitted up for the fete. There was

also a plentiful supply of Dublin stout and Devonshire cider. At five o'clock supper was on the table, substantial good old English fare, roast beef and plum pudding. Tremendous cheering followed by "all hands" for long life and happiness to the family who had so liberally entertained them.'

This school of Mrs Brunel's was clearly a stop-gap, destined to be followed up by a much more elaborate form of social provision. Among the bungalows of modern Barton there stands a building of Victorian date bearing a blue plaque erected by the Torbay Civic Society. It records:

BARN CLOSE
AN ESTATE OF
HOMES, SCHOOL & CHAPEL
PLANNED FOR HIS
WORKERS BY
I.K. BRUNEL
1806-1859

Like Watcombe Park this was an ambition that was not fully achieved – yet its conception is a tribute to some of the lesser-known qualities of this remarkable man. Somewhere in this unpromising area he needed homes for his key-workers. We know much about its decayed state from the descriptions in

Lady Thomas, Brunel's great great granddaughter, reading plaque at Barn Close
Image: Helen Hillard

Edmund Gosse's *Father and Son*. The Gosse family settled in St. Marychurch in 1857, and Edmund would be walked to Pavor, ('decayed almost to extinction'), and on to Barton with its 'desultry street of ancient detached cottages.' What saved Barton was its setting in the hills and the rambling plants of its semi-wild gardens. It was a 'bower', young Edmund decided, 'in vivid contrast to our own harsh, open, squalid village [St. Marychurch], with its mean modern houses, its absence of all vegetation…Around and beyond Barton there lay fairyland. All was mysterious, unexplored, rich with infinite possibilities…' One such possibility was to be this model workers' village, repeating on a small scale the provision already made for railway families at Swindon. Improved housing was sorely needed in Torquay. Sumptuous villas were spreading across the hillsides of the Warberries and the Lincombes: those who were building and servicing them dossed down where they could. Many

slept in common lodging houses or the attics of beer-houses - anywhere they could find space in the crowded slums of George Street, Madrepore and Pimlico. There were serious outbreaks of cholera, leading to an early example of town-planning in the Victoria Park area, laid out like a military camp.

Securing good workers' housing – 'artisan housing' in the jargon of the day – was an enthusiasm which Brunel shared with the Prince. One of the great successes – and crowd-drawers – of the 1851 Exhibition was the row of Model Dwelling-houses, sponsored by Prince Albert himself. Among his various contributions to the Exhibition, Brunel had been appointed Chairman and Reporter for Class VII – Civil Engineering, Architecture, and Building Contrivances. The Jury awarded the Council's Medal to Paxton, designer of the Crystal Palace itself: but a second Medal was awarded to Prince Albert, 'as the exhibitor of this most useful and interesting contribution to the Exhibition, and to whom the nation at large is so deeply indebted for the promotion of this important subject.' A collection of letters and documents among the Royal Archives at Windsor bear testimony to the depth of the Prince's involvement. On New Year's Day, 1851, he was writing to Lord Ashley about finding a suitable site for a row of Model Lodging Houses. The modest purpose was to make them available 'for the inspection of such visitors to the Exhibition as may wish to visit them.'

After complex negotiations involving the Duke of Wellington a site was found, and the interest in the houses exceeded all expectations. A full report was made to the Prince in October. The houses had been inspected by 250,000 persons – over 7,400 on one day alone. 'The principle of construction, and materials used for the floors, have therefore been subjected to a severe test.'

The fervour of Brunel's Report indicates his deep and genuine involvement in the topic:

'To place, within reach of all, a large proportion of those comforts most conducive to health, to habits of cleanliness and decency, which have hitherto been enjoyed as luxuries only by the few; to remove that painful necessity under which the poor man now labours of submitting to privations and inconveniences, which are destructive of moral habits and utterly inconsistent with domestic comfort, and to place at his command a certain degree almost of luxury, which tends to refine the mind, and substitutes a comfortable home for a miserable and barely efficient shelter from the elements, is the ambitious but wise and benevolent design of those who, with the example and under the leadership of HIS ROYAL HIGHNESS PRINCE ALBERT, have of late actively promoted the improvement of the dwellings of the working-class…It is difficult to over-estimate the magnitude and importance of the effects of such a change upon the population of the country, whether as adding to their individual happiness, or improving their physical and moral condition, and thus rendering them more valuable and useful members of society.'

Brunel must have swallowed his earlier powerful objections to the award of either medals or money prizes to exhibitors. As Adrian Vaughan has pointed out, 'he felt that the glory of being in the Exhibition was reward enough.' He also foresaw the basic difficulty confronted by all such awarding bodies – often described as the problem of comparing apples with pears. So vehement was his opposition that he wrote a powerful letter to Prince Albert: 'I strongly disapprove of any prizes being offered. It is quite unnecessary…there are an infinity of shades of merit…'

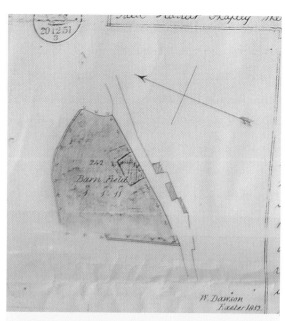

In March 1852 Brunel bought a field of just under two acres in the village of Barton for £250. The site was in the awkward shape of a half circle, but he turned this to an advantage by planning to build his houses in a crescent. © *Devon Record Office*

Though forced to swallow the notion of medals, Brunel stuck to his guns at first over the question of accepting any financial reward for his considerable contribution to the success of the Exhibition. The correspondence shows that he was finally swayed only by the consideration that a refusal on his part would create difficulties for the others who were to be rewarded. He may also have realised that his honorarium could be used to finance a practical example of that 'wise and benevolent design' that he had so recently applauded. In March 1852 he bought a field of just under two acres in the village of Barton for £250. The site was in the awkward shape of a half circle, but Brunel turned this to an advantage by planning to build his houses in a crescent. Along the circumference ten semi-detached cottages would be built – very large by existing standards and almost certainly designed by Brunel himself. It seems that they incorporated elements of cross-bracing as used in his ship designs. This permitted more slender masonry for the walls, and hence a larger building for the same expenditure. Only four cottages were built in Brunel's lifetime - until his future home at Watcombe was completed there was probably no need for them. But the four that were built still provide a very acceptable standard of housing a century and a half later.

Along the diameter of the half-circle and adjacent to the public road would lie the combined school and chapel. This, too, was probably designed by Brunel: such

Only four cottages were built at Barn Close in Brunel's lifetime - until his future home at Watcombe was completed there was probably no need for them. But the four that were built still provide a very acceptable standard of housing a century and a half later. Image: Helen Hillard

St Augustines Church 1882 - the Combined School and Chapel, planned by Brunel for the Barn Close development, was built by his wife and sons after his death and presented to the parish of St Marychurch © Devon Record Office

buildings appear in his sketch-books. As with the remaining cottages this was not erected during Brunel's lifetime, and it was many years before the family finances were in a sufficiently settled state to push ahead with the venture. On 27th August 1874 – nearly fifteen years after his father's death – Henry wrote to his brother outlining the proposal and including a rough sketch of the site. The following year the land was presented to the Vicar and Churchwardens of St. Marychurch under the terms of the Education Act (1870). It was to be used 'for a school for the education of children and adults or children only of the labouring, manufacturing and other poor classes.' By 1878 Harrod's Royal County Directory of Devonshire recorded that 'at Barton a mission chapel has recently been erected, which is also used as a school.' In recent years the building has been converted to two dwelling-houses, but its unmistakeable outline remains. The Torbay Civic Society's blue plaque is fixed to the entrance porch through which hundreds of Barton children must have passed into school. A Civic Society leaflet tells the story of this project

In recent years the building has been converted to two dwelling-houses, but its unmistakeable outline remains   Image: Peter Lemar

under the title: '**Barn Close – Isambard Kingdom Brunel as the Good Employer.**'

Environmental Champion

A major problem for Torquay, bounded by the sea on one side, and ringed by hills, was where to site essential services such as gasworks. The extension of the railway to Newton Abbot and Torquay had sparked a housing-boom. The owners or tenants of the new property demanded the convenience of gas-lighting – and supplies were running out. Since 1834 the town had been supplied from a small gas-works sited alongside the Babbacombe Road, just above the elegant Torwood Gardens. Quite apart from the deficiency of supply, the juxtaposition of gas-works and public gardens was unacceptable. The slopes above were dotted with new villas, and their occupiers resented the presence of a gas-works in the foreground of the promised 'extensive sea views'. Now a new company was proposed which would build a larger works …but where? The Cary family – one of the two big local landowners – offered a site at Babbacombe Beach, just where Queen Victoria had revelled in the scenery a few years earlier. This site would have two advantages: it would place this essential but unseemly neighbour well away from other Cary property; and the works could be provided with sea-borne coal, thus reducing its running costs.

Here was an early example of those environmental disputes which have now

Babbacombe, as Queen Victoria had noted, was one of the jewels in Torquay's crown. When he heard of the proposal to site a gas works there, Brunel was strongly opposed to this assault on the local scenery and joined the campaign, using his opinion and great influence, to succeed in 'driving the nuisance from Babbacombe.'

become so common in our overcrowded island. Babbacombe, as the Queen herself had noted, was one of the jewels in Torquay's crown. A furious row broke out between the developer and the conservationists, and Brunel was approached to play his part in combating this threatened 'nuisance'. In June 1854 he received a letter from Rev. Alexander Watson, Vicar of St. Marychurch, asking him to join the battle – an invitation to which he replied with great caution. To begin with, he insisted on having an accurate briefing. 'I am a terribly matter of fact man, and never like moving in a fog – or in other words I like to know exactly all the *facts* in any matter in which I do move – and I only call a *fact* - a statement every word of which is capable of rigid proof.' Having defined himself as a man of precision he went on to disclose a genuine horror at the proposal. 'I had understood from Mr. Kitson the other day that it was proposed by the Carys to put the gasworks on Babbacombe Beach and that I expressed my astonishment at the inhabitants of the whole neighbourhood not violently protesting against it and opposing it.'

Brunel went on to express his reluctance to become engaged. 'I wish I lived near enough to take a party in the opposition but I must not. I could not pretend that it would annoy me – and they are not likely to come into my valley – but I will send you exact particulars of what can best be done.' Babbacombe Beach was about a mile and a half away from Watcombe, so neither sight nor scent of the gasworks would have been offensive to Brunel's property: but he appears to have been strongly opposed to this assault on the local scenery. Nor, as he first proposed, was he simply lurking in the background supplying technical advice. As with the Battle of Mickleton Tunnel - where Brunel had led an army of navvies – and other episodes, Brunel was not the man to stand aside if a good fight was in prospect. He was like the war-horse in the Book of Job: 'He saith among the trumpets, Ha, ha; and he smelleth the battle afar off, the thunder of the captains, and the shouting.'

Time was short. The Gas Bill was due for debate in the House of Lords Committee the following month, and a Public Meeting was called to plan the opposition. The assembly selected Brunel and Mr. March Phillips – another ardent conservationist – to act as principal witnesses for the opposition. At the Committee hearing the promoters argued strongly that the need was pressing because of frequent public complaints about the present Torwood Gardens site; but Brunel produced a conclusive counter-argument. There was no point, he maintained, in moving the gasworks from its present unsatisfactory site to another that would prove equally objectionable. Better to leave it where it was until a suitable site could be located. Brunel's well-presented arguments prevailed, as recorded in the local newspaper: 'Mr. Brunel however, followed, and succeeded, by the expression of his opinion and great influence, in driving the nuisance from Babbacombe.'

This was no mean victory and had lasting effects. Brunel's oratory in the Lords had ensured that the whole Babbacombe area was now permanently safe from the threat of any future gasworks.

The amended Bill ensured that any new works must be sited to the West of the town, between Torquay and Paignton. Since Cockington and Chelston were still closed to development, the only possible site was close to the sea at Hollacombe. Babbacombe's gain was Hollacombe's loss, and gas was produced there for a century, until North Sea Gas could be piped in (under Cockington) and the gasholders could be removed from the seaward portion of the site. Their foundations have been landscaped to form an award-winning public garden – a conservation success which Brunel would no doubt have applauded.

Social Complexities

Brunel's planned estate building was rendered more difficult by the many forms of social unrest then stirring in both town and countryside. The Bread Riots of 1847 – the year that Brunel first came to Watcombe – must have left a legacy of bitterness with over seventy imprisoned and two transported. A more tenacious obstacle to his plans was the presence in the district of a group of small – but stubborn – landowners. They resulted from the idealistic activities of Rev. George M. Coleridge, Vicar of St. Marychurch from 1827-47, who was a strong supporter of the Allotments Movement. This movement, backed by the Labourers Friend Society, had the initial object of encouraging country labourers to support themselves and the families through their work on the land, rather than become a burden on the Poor Rates. From 1830 until her death in 1845, Mary Ann Gilbert of Eastbourne conducted an elaborate series of well-researched experiments, to demonstrate what could be achieved. (As part of her publicity she sent potatoes grown by her methods to Lord Liverpool, and also won the support of the reformer Sidney Smith.) Her husband, Davies Gilbert, (last President of the Board of Agriculture), was a Cornishman: the family paid frequent visits to the West Country and Ann Gilbert's ideas won widespread backing.

Around St. Marychurch Rev. Coleridge's ideas went beyond keeping labourers off the Poor Rates: he aimed to spread ownership of land more widely in order to create a peasantry on the French model. By the time Brunel arrived upon the scene he found himself confronted – and to some extent surrounded – by an entrenched structure of small proprietors, proud to use the old title of yeoman. He may have been a man of almost irresistible force, but here he came upon the immovable object. A large landowner such as Henry Langford Brown was willing to sell a large block of land to subsidise his yachting, but the local yeomen could be moved by no such temptations. A glaring example of this immovability appears on the Watcombe Estate map of 1859: a finger of land called Codner's Piece pokes in an inconvenient – almost insulting – fashion into the heart of Brunel's parkland. Clearly neither Brunel's persuasive arguments nor the

lure of gold sovereigns had eased Codner's stubborn hold upon his acres.

This was not the only instance of local yeomen exercising a stubborn grip. Closely allied to the Allotment Movement was the campaign to preserve Common Rights. Defence of common land was becoming an important national issue, resulting in 1865 in the formation of The Commons Preservation Society – quick to flex its muscles against infringers of age-old rights. (The very next year Augustus Smith – 'Emperor of the Scillies' – despatched a large force of navvies by special train to demolish two miles of illegal fencing on Berkhamsted Common.) Thirteen years earlier, in 1853, an interesting battle took place on Brunel's own doorstep at Watcombe Common. This tract of land below Giant Rock was shared by four owners - one of them Brunel – but local farmers had

Section of the 1859 Estate Map showing the strip of land Codner refused to sell to Brunel.
© Devon Record Office

MUSICAL FETE CHAMPETRE AT WATCOMBE, NEAR TORQUAY.

Musical Fete Champetre at Watcombe near Torquay from The Illustrated London News August 14th 1852
© The Illustrated London News

grazing rights and the local public had free access. It was a great place for local gatherings. In 1849 a large party of tradesmen had a picnic there, and in 1851 it was the turn of the Mechanics Institute: by July 1852 there was the first Fete Champetre. This must have been a success, for in August 1853 the Torquay Choral Society arranged a spectacular Grand Gala & Fete Champetre on the Common. (This was the month before Mrs Brunel staged her party for the estate workers, so the family was probably in residence at the time.)

The lavish spectacle is an example of how quickly people took advantage of the new railways. Sidney Smith had deplored that England had no amusements other than vice and religion: railways and Thomas Cook changed all that.

Soon there were outings, visits to the seaside, and 'events', such as that at Watcombe. The line had reached Torquay less than five years earlier, but now as many as 7,000 people are reckoned to have attended this event, some by special trains from as far afield as Bristol and Birmingham. Arriving at

Torre Station, most would have had to walk three miles to reach Watcombe Common. There they listened to a choir of 1,000 voices, watched a sports meeting and a military tattoo. The face of Giant Rock was floodlit, and as a Grand Finale the band of a Highland Regiment lined the top to beat Retreat. Presumably Brunel and the other owners had given their permission, but the organizers had not reckoned with the Commoners. One of the local yeomen, George Nickels, disputed the right of outsiders to fence off the Common. He and his supporters arrived with axes, demolished the barriers, and invited the oncoming crowds to enter without payment: thus a superb spectacle became a financial disaster! The outcome was that 'Farmer George' Nickels maintained for the public the free use of Watcombe Common - in June 1856 there was 'Peace Rejoicing' there at the end of the Crimean War. Public rights at Watcombe Common were carefully preserved when the land was purchased in 1935 by Torquay Council. There was free public access to the Coastal Footpath to Maidencombe, which was opened just before the Second World War.

Brunels at the Poultry-show

A study of the local paper confirms that the Brunels differed from many of today's owners of second homes – accused of coming to live in an area without making any contribution to it. As early as 1852 Mrs Brunel was noted as winning First Prize for Bantams at the June Horticultural Show. This was only a start. By December Brunel himself had been roped in as Patron of the forthcoming Poultry Exhibition, to be held in January 1853. By now the family must have developed a fair-sized enterprise at Watcombe Villa, for they won First Prize for a Silver Poland, and Second Prizes for 'Best Devon Pen', Malay, Game Fowls and Geese. By 1854 the Brunels were winning awards or commendations for Dorkings, Game Fowls, Polands, Silver Pencil Hamburghs and Turkeys. (Such success produced an exception to the general rule that 'all publicity is good publicity': the paper also reported that one of Mrs Brunel's festive turkeys had been stolen.) How much feeding and pampering of the poultry was performed by Brunel and his wife in person is of course uncertain; there exists, however, ample proof of an intention to engage with the life of the neighbourhood. Mary Brunel features in many accounts of Regatta and New Year Balls. She made many friends in the area, and it is significant how frequently she visited the area – sometimes for long periods – following her husband's death.

CHAPTER 6:
'My unfortunate friend, Mr. Watson...'

Watson's building schemes falter

Brunel's involvement in the crisis at St. Marychurch Parish Church is one of the strangest episodes in his career. In 1854 he worked closely with Rev. Alexander Watson in opposing the threatened gasworks at Babbacombe. Though reluctant at first to become too deeply involved, he was converted to an active role - partly by his innate love of a scrap, but perhaps also by a certain respect for Watson himself, whom he later described several times as 'a friend'. Brunel must already have had some contact with Watson as his vicar, but fighting shoulder to shoulder in 'The Battle of the Gasworks' the two men had possibly developed some of the comradeship of old soldiers. Watson had an interesting background. He was the son of Joseph Watson, nephew of Thomas Braidwood, who established in 1760 in Edinburgh the first school for the Deaf in Britain. In 1783 the school moved to London, and by now Joseph Watson was in charge: in 1809 he published a text book, *Instruction of the Deaf and Dumb*. (The school's repute reached the United States. In 1815 - once Britain and America were no longer at war - Thomas Hopkins Gallaudet came to London to gain the technical knowledge to establish a similar school across the Atlantic.)

Alexander Watson, then, grew up in a family environment with plentiful contact with wealthy philanthropists, and where there was considerable éclat: much of his subsequent misfortune may have been caused by an ambition to compete with his father and 'cut a dash' in his own field. For a time he had a curacy at Cheltenham where he seems to have laboured successfully and become popular: it was after moving further West to become Vicar of St. Marychurch in 1851 that his woes began. It was just a year after Cardinal Wiseman had come to England to become Archbishop of Westminster. Anti-Catholic feeling was then at its strongest. (Thomas Carlyle wrote to his brother: 'The flagstones and walls are all chalked "No Popery!" "Burn the Pope!"; "Kick the Pope's bottom!" etc. etc.') Alexander Watson was devoted to High Church ritual, and before long his local nickname was 'Candlestick Watson'. As a result about half his congregation voted with their feet – and their purses – and established a Free Episcopal church nearby at Furrough Cross in 1853. (Above the hall door appears the Gladstone family arms: one of the first ministers was cousin to the future Prime Minister.) Furrough Cross was soon in the thick of religious controversy: a frequent preacher was the Rev. James Shore of the Free Church at

Bridgetown Totnes, who had been imprisoned on the prosecution of the Bishop of Exeter, Henry Philpotts. Shore was backed by his local magnate, the Duke of Somerset, and this dispute between bishop and peer became a cause celebre.

Having lost half his congregation, this was not perhaps the most propitious of moments for Watson to set about a major rebuilding of the parish church! Partly he seems to have been inspired by Laudian doctrines, and wished to provide a building that expressed 'the Beauty of Holiness': partly he may have wished to show his departed parishioners that the church could flourish without them. On the other hand urgent remedial work may have been required, for twenty years earlier a Professor of Architecture, Mr. R. Brown, had written a damning report on the condition of the church. The columns in the south aisle were ten inches out of the perpendicular and 'propped against the wall by the most unsightly pieces of wood – truly disgraceful.' The three galleries were described by Brown as the worst he had ever seen. The oldest, erected in 1732, was described as in a tottering state, and having 'all the appearances, from the burlesque paintings on it, of having been part of the gallery of a country theatre. This may appear lightly spoken, but such is the case.' Brown was also critical of the all-pervading damp: 'Although no church in Devonshire is higher situated, I never entered one that is so damp and cold...Why do the clergy not get stoves in their churches and mats laid down in their aisles as they have in London?' So damp and slippery were the flagstones within the altar rails that an earlier Vicar, Edward Kitson, had fallen heavily while performing his office. A tablet on the south wall recorded that his death in 1827 resulted from this fall.

Alexander Watson was appointed Vicar of St. Marychurch in 1851, and must have been determined to put matters right without delay. As early as March 1852 a circular was published appealing for funds and some work was begun, as reported in a contemporary guidebook to Torquay and District. According to this account the ancient structure 'was defaced by wretched galleries, ruinous pews, and various other modern abominations. Besides all this, it was in the highest degree damp and out of repair. During the incumbency of the present energetic vicar, (Rev. A. Watson), the chancel has been entirely re-built in the best possible taste, reflecting great credit on all parties concerned in the restoration.' So far, so good; but the rebuilding of the chancel seems to have been carried out without any thought of how this would relate to other portions of the fabric. 'It appears, however, that the scale on which it has been done causes the older part of the church to present so mean and contracted an appearance as to necessitate the demolition of the whole, and its re-erection on a scale and in a style proportionate to that of the new portion of the church when the requisite funds can be obtained.'

Watson's well-meaning intervention seems to have caused as much harm as good to the building's fabric: a report by the architect Hugall (17th March 1859) pronounced that the building was dangerous. Yet another building programme was put in hand, which was only completed when the new tower was dedicated in 1877 (Apart from this tower, the church was destroyed during a German bombing raid in May 1943.)

Brunel to the rescue

Brunel, then, was involved with Alexander Watson's earlier partial rebuilding, showing that he was among those of the congregation who remained loyal to the vicar. There has been speculation on the nature of Brunel's religious beliefs. Angus Buchanan, (*Brunel*, 2002) concludes that 'he observed the proprieties of

Brunel became involved in the restoration of St Marychurch Parish Church - giving his time on the building committee and making several generous donations © Torquay Museum

attendance at the Church of England when he was able to do so.' He also kept Sundays free from professional commitments wherever possible. (Two of those close to him, his wife Mary and her brother, John Horsley, were both devout Anglicans, and their influence was probably important) Another factor was the Victorian convention that squire and parson should work in harmony wherever possible: if the church needed rebuilding, then it was Brunel's duty to apply his engineering and managerial talents – and also his purse - to the task. It is on record that Brunel made a *second* donation of £200: probably this had been preceded by at least a similar sum. At about this time Brunel was elected to the Building Committee, and events were to show that he was no mere figurehead.

The crisis broke early in 1856. By now a new vicar, Henry Newland, had been appointed, Watson having moved on to the West Devon village of Bridestowe in September 1855. Soon it became apparent that the parish was likely to be saddled with the debts resulting from his ambitious efforts at St. Marychurch. (Strictly the debt was owed by Rev. Watson personally, but in practice parishioners seem to have felt morally obliged to extricate him from the pit he had dug for himself: and nobody seems to have felt this more strongly than Brunel himself.) What followed is a fine illustration of the old adage: 'if you want a job well done, then find a busy person to do it.' Brunel was more than fully occupied with his railways, bridges and other engineering projects, and with the gigantic problems of the *Great Eastern*: he was also turning his thoughts to the building of his house at Watcombe. In addition he later became a very sick man. Yet for nearly three years – from February 1856 to December 1858 – he devoted his considerable powers of negotiation and persuasion in the interests of the feckless Watson.

Here are just a few samples of the many forceful letters written on Watson's behalf to some of his creditors and their lawyers:

The Great Eastern under construction. At the time, this was the biggest ship in the world. © Science & Society

25th February, 1856: 'I have received a letter from my friend, the Rev. Mr. Watson of Bridestowe, by which I learn you have served him with a writ…'

29th February, 1856: (To Luccombe and Pince, the well-known nurserymen of Exeter.) 'I feel bound to tell you that your account…appears to me exceptionally large for the work done, and the small amount of planting that I ever saw has nearly all failed.' (On 3rd June 1856 Brunel sent Watson a personal gift, of £100)

14th November, 1856: 'As one of [Mr. Watson's] parishioners I have told him that I will do my best to relieve him from the consequences of his improvidence in the building of the church.'

18th November, 1856: '…I trust I may be able to save your client and my unfortunate friend, Mr. Watson, from the necessity of a law suit.'

1st December, 1858: 'I have something to propose which must be at least better for your client than the nothing which I very much fear must otherwise be the limit of his hopes…We are now going to make an effort to raise something for your client if he is wise enough to take what he can get. The past subscription has been raised with difficulty, as the burden falls upon few. I want to know if you will settle for £250. I shall not attempt to raise more, and I leave England for Egypt for the winter on Saturday morning, and when I am gone I fear little could be done…'

3rd December, 1858: 'I have settled with Darby's solicitors for £250. I don't know what funds you have, you must put me down for what you think right…'

By now Brunel had been diagnosed as suffering from Bright's disease, (Nephritis), and had been ordered away by his doctors in a vain effort to recover his health. Nine months later he was dead, so this settlement of the parish debt was probably the final service he was able to render to his Devonshire neighbours. It illustrates the powerful commitment he felt towards the parish where he intended to make his home: ownership of Watcombe imposed obligations as well as providing pleasures. In addition Brunel was frequently pointing out to his engineers and others, that there were certain ways in which a 'gentleman' was expected to behave, and mid-Victorian England gave much emphasis to the Christian duty of aiding those in trouble. The very year, 1856, that Brunel began his rescue-mission was the year when Charles Kingsley wrote to Tom Hughes the oft-quoted lines in 'The Invitation':

> 'Do the work that's nearest,
> Though it's dull at whiles,
> Helping, when we meet them,
> Lame dogs over stiles.'

Watson's sorry fate

Brunel seems to have looked on the unfortunate Watson as one of these lame dogs - improvident and over-ambitious rather than fully blameworthy. Napoleon used to inquire of his generals: 'is he lucky?' One cannot now be certain whether Watson was to some extent unlucky, or whether he was mainly the architect of his own misfortunes.

On leaving St. Marychurch he staggered from one crisis to another. At Bridestowe he engaged in a further experiment in costly alterations. From the large display advertisements he inserted in newspapers, it seems he intended to finance the work by developing an income as a tutor. Before any sufficient income had appeared he was removed from Bridestowe because of his debts: next he was involved in a Chancery suit over his London chapel – readers of Dickens will appreciate how disastrous this would have been! Watson's life might well have added a further example to the sorry list of misfortunes in Johnson's *The Vanity of Human Wishes*:

> 'There mark what ills the
> scholar's life assail,
> Toil, envy, want, the patron,
> and the jail.'

His career, once so promising, degenerated into a series of curacies in England and France. His days ended as curate in a remote parish in Yorkshire, Middleton on the Wolds. There, during the bitter winter of February 1865, he fell on an icy road, dying soon after of pneumonia at the age of fifty.

CHAPTER 7:
1858 - Watcombe planning still moving forward

'I will build a house…'

During the early stages of the Watson imbroglio Brunel was showing signs of turning early dreams and paper plans into reality: he would make a start on the building of his house. In 1887 a reporter for the *Gardeners' Chronicle* summarised how Brunel had planned to go about his estate-building. 'About 1848 Mr. Brunel, who evidently had an eye for something besides tunnels and big ships, was so impressed with the natural beauties which the place presented that he bought the land with the object of having it laid out and building a house thereon. Acting on the principle that while men are sleeping trees are growing, he took the wise course of having the ground-work and the planting done before beginning to build…' Landscaping, then, would come first: but while planning his garden and woodlands – many aspects of which are dotted around in his Sketchbooks – Brunel was also mulling over the form his house would take. It was a confusing period in which to come to a decision. Some elements of 18th Century Classicism lingered: 'Oaklands' at Okehampton is an example, with its Ionic porticoes. In and around Torquay, in accord with the wish to resemble the Bay of Naples, Italianate designs

remained in vogue for much of the century. But Gothic was also making an entry – 'Luscombe' at Dawlish, designed by John Nash for the Hoare family, is a case in point. Brunel's railway architecture never formed a consistent style, with Classical tunnel arches leading on to a Mock-Tudor station at Bristol. His sketchbooks show him considering different options for his future home, as well described by Rolt. 'Brunel at first sketched for himself a Gothic castle with a great turret tower brooding over the sea, but, as he probably realised, this was better suited to some colder and more savage coast than that of South Devon. It was soon relegated in favour of a design for an Italianate villa with a belvedere and a colonnaded terrace.'

Perhaps Brunel decided in the end to 'play safe'. In 1851 he commissioned a design, in what has been described as the Loire Valley chateau style, from the leading country-house architect, William Burn, 1789-1870. (Some of William Burn's drawings for Watcombe are in the R.I.B.A. Library, and some have been deposited in the Bristol University collection.) A Scot, and son of an architect father, Burn trained under Sir Robert Smirke, designer of the British Museum. At first Burn practised in

Watcombe Plans: front and rear elevations showing turret towers
© *University of Bristol*

Watcombe Plans: west elevation showing turret towers, window details and garden room
© University of Bristol

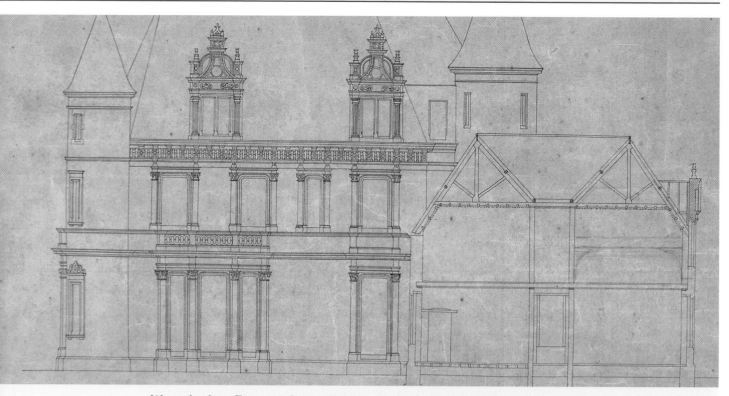

Watcombe plans: East wing showing elaborate window heads and cornices
© University of Bristol

Edinburgh, where he initiated the Scottish Baronial style; but in 1844, already in his mid-fifties, he set up a practice in London. Soon he was winning commissions all round the country – his Octagon Drawing-Room at 'Raby Castle', County Durham, is one of his many accomplishments. Two houses Burn was designing at this time illustrate how 'new money' was again starting to flood in to irrigate the building of country houses: at 'Orwell Park' Suffolk, (1851-53), Colonel George Tomline's 'fortuitous inheritance' financed a massive extension; in neighbouring Norfolk, at 'Lynford', Lyne Stephens used a fortune inherited from Lisbon trade to spend £145,000 on a new mansion in Jacobean style.

Brunel, of course, possessed no inherited wealth: thirty years earlier his father had been arrested for debt and confined to the King's Bench prison! The financing of house and estate depended entirely on his earnings as engineer, but these were substantial enough to place him on a footing with many of the landed gentry. This was neatly illustrated when William Burn died in 1870 at the end of a long working career. A list of his clients was attached to his obituary: Brunel's name appears between the Earl of Hamilton and the Earl of Montrose, evidence of his firm intention that leading engineers should now be numbered among the aristocrats. Inevitably there were risks when houses were built unsupported by landed income. Nearly a century earlier the raffish John Byng had pointed to the

unwisdom of men of fifty not buying 'a place ready cut and dry'd.' Instead they built new and then died leaving their heirs burdened with great houses but lacking an income to support them. Such was the sorry fate of many houses based on the sudden wealth derived from political place, naval prize money, or the profits of the law. The future of Brunel's house at Watcombe would rest partly on his engineering genius, but partly on the less substantial foundation of bodily health and strength.

It was in May 1855, after completing his prefabricated hospital for the Crimea, that Brunel first showed a firm intention of starting on his home. He wrote to quarry owner, Wylam Walker of Hexham, Northumberland, seeking his advice on the best type of stone for facing his house. 'The stone I may require is for facing a house and for cornices, mouldings etc. with a good deal of work upon them...If you can assume a moderate sized country house say 88 ft. square with bold and deep cornices, window dressing and rather elaborate window heads you will know the sort of stone required. I have left the option to the builder of using Bath stone or yours, and I should prefer yours.' Despite the expense of sea-transport, Walker's stone from the Prudham quarries would provide a better finish. This was the stone used for Barnes Bridge in London, and Queen Victoria chose it for the new stable-block at 'Claremont House'. (Such insistence on quality would have considerably increased the cost of

William Burn's 1851 design for Watcombe
© RIBA

Brunel Manor 2005
© Tracey Elliot-Reep

Brunel's house. The figure would probably be well beyond the £15,000 to £20,000 estimated for a house of his proposed dimensions in the 1850's.) Further negotiations with Walker followed, yet when Brunel died four years later no more than the foundations and cellars of his house had been completed. Why the delay? No doubt a major reason was the protracted, wearying - and costly – struggle to complete and launch *Great Eastern*. But building plans were not entirely shelved: on 13th March 1856 the sum of £159.5.0 was paid to quantity-surveyor George Martin of '85 Baker Street', Portman Square: 'the amount of your account in connection with proposed house at Watcombe.' At that time plans were clearly moving ahead.

Yet another indication of Brunel's resolve to make a start on the house was the presence at Watcombe, in the autumn of 1857, of Brunel's brother-in-law, John Horsley. By now Brunel had been forced to leave 'Watcombe Villa' at the foot of his estate. There was correspondence in 1855 about new leasing arrangements and by December 1856 the house was offered for sale: 'now occupied by I.K. Brunel who is about to leave.' (For a time he and his wife had toyed with the idea of purchasing the house, but presumably it would have been an extravagance to lay out capital on property at a time when they were about to start work at Watcombe.) So in March 1857 the Brunels moved to 'Portland Villa' at the top of the hill. It was considerably smaller than 'Watcombe Villa', but quite

Section of estate map of 1859 showing site of house
© Devon Record Office

suitable as a temporary home. As the name suggests, one of its attractions was the view across Lyme Bay to the cliffs of Portland. A few hundred yards away, down the lane leading to Maidencombe was a large villa named 'Oarstone [now Orestone] Lodge', and this was rented for several months by the Horsleys. Living at such close quarters the two families would have ample opportunity to discuss their respective building plans: Horsley was then in the early stages of scheming his future country house that was to materialise at Cranbrook in Kent at the hands of Norman Shaw.

'…the happiest hours of his life…'

The autumn of 1857 was a busy time for Brunel, with the planned launch of *Great Eastern* fast approaching. In June he had promised the Directors a launch in

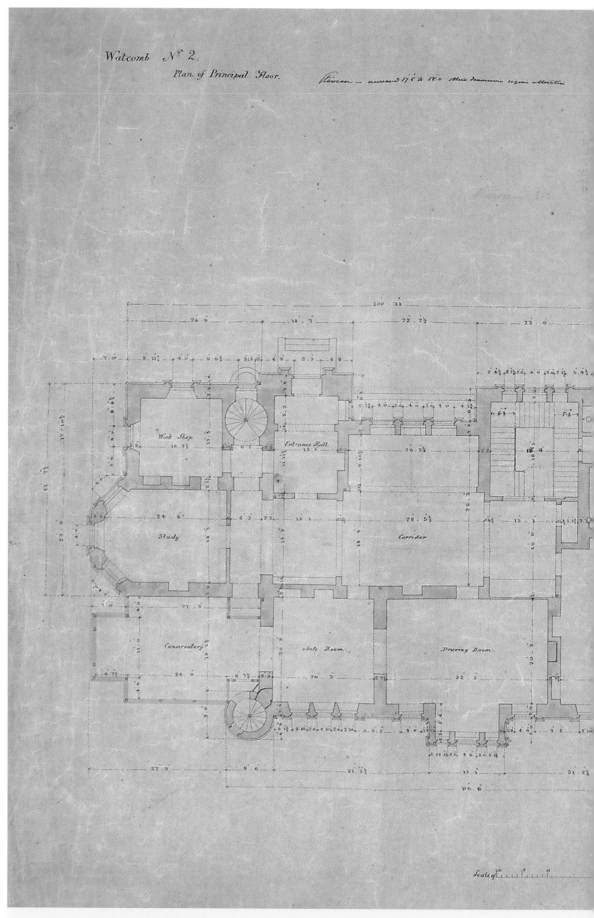

Brunel's plans for the ground floor
© *University of Bristol*

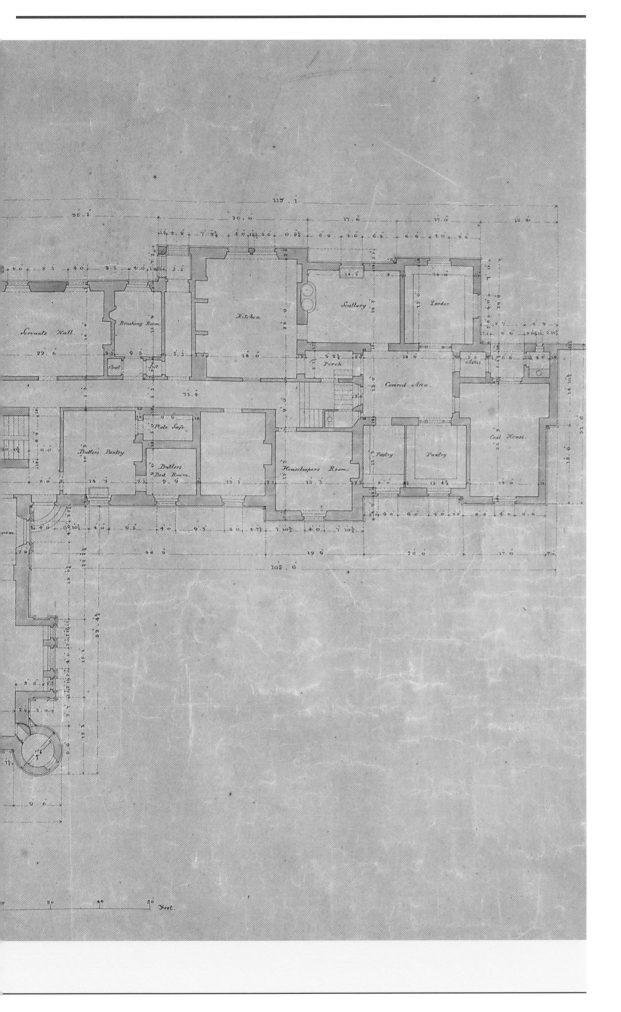

Watcomb   N.º 3.

Plan of Principal Bed Room Floor.

Dressing Room.   Mrs Brunel's
                      Dressing Rm

Family Bed Room.   Bath Room.   Bed Room.   Bed Room.

                                        Corridor.

                      Boudoir.   Dress.ʳ Rm   Bed Room.

Brunel's plans for the 1st floor
© University of Bristol

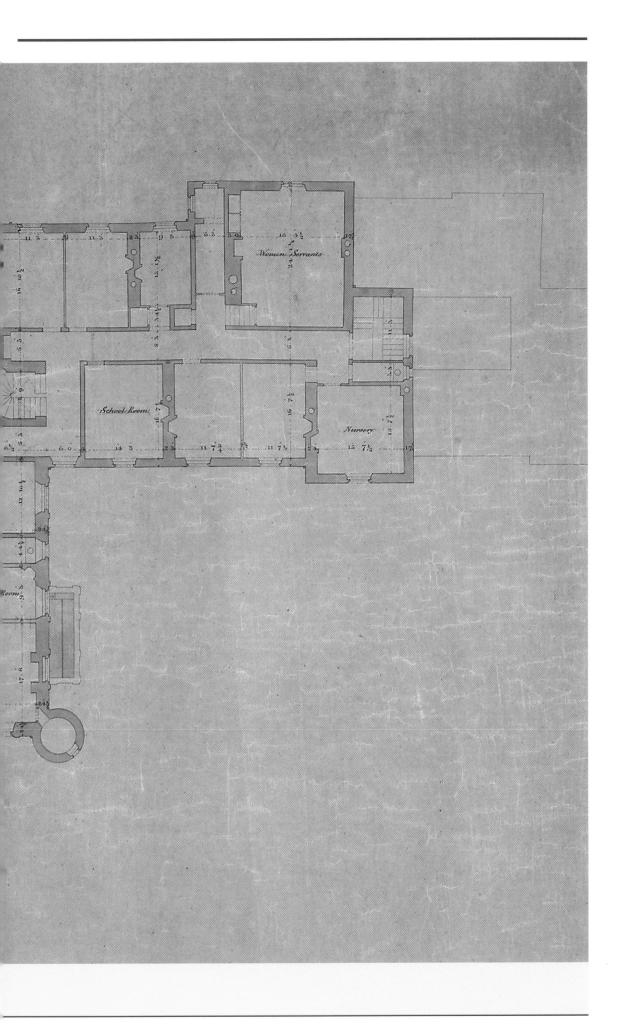

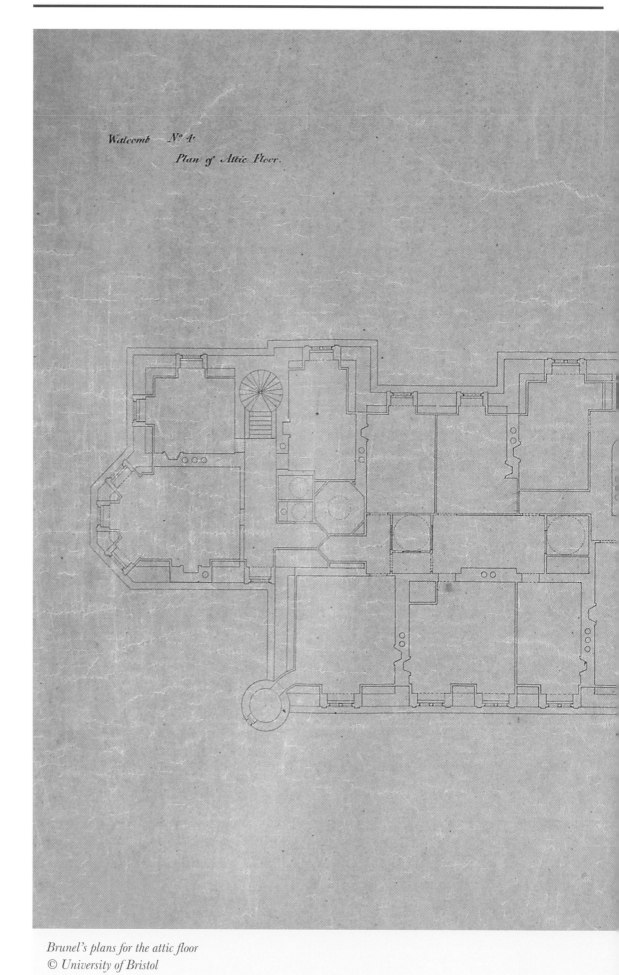

Witcomb № 4·

Plan of Attic Floor.

Brunel's plans for the attic floor
© University of Bristol

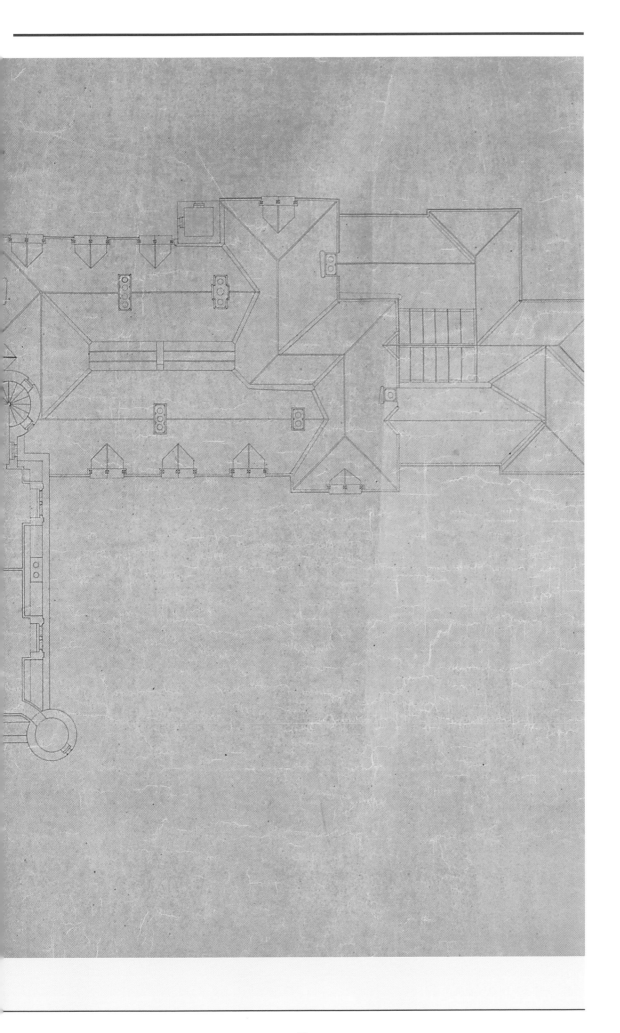

August, but construction problems and delays with the launching ways led to postponements. It was not until 3rd November that the failed attempt took place: and not until 31st January 1858 – with the aid of a battery of hydraulic presses - that the ship finally floated clear on the Thames. Rolt's biography presents a picture of a man almost insane with worry – living almost day and night in the shipyard. – all thoughts of Watcombe driven out of his mind. That Watcombe was still very much in Brunel's mind is proved by two letters written towards the end of October 1857 to his somewhat bothersome neighbour, Daniel Woodley. Woodley also had plenty of troubles on his mind, for the marble business launched by his father in 1806 was now on a downward spiral. For many years it had a large export trade – as far as Australia – as well as a flourishing home market. The Woodleys invested heavily in both housing and land, and by the time Brunel arrived on the scene in 1847 they already owned extensive property.

At first Brunel co-operated with Woodley in an exchange of land to improve access to their respective holdings: several letters exist in which Brunel discusses in friendly fashion how the new roads may be laid out to their mutual advantage. Then relations deteriorated, partly, no doubt, because both men were harassed with business worries. Woodley's fortunes reached their peak about the

Excerpt from Brunel's letter of October 1857 to Daniel Woodley
© University of Bristol

time of the Great Exhibition of 1851, when the firm won several prizes: the following year, when Prince Albert visited Babbacombe Bay, he honoured Woodley by visiting his showroom at St. Marychurch. But the firm was over-reaching itself, and by the later 1850's Woodley's land was heavily mortgaged. Soon afterwards the marble business was taken over by Harry Grant. By 1863 Woodley was involved in bankruptcy proceedings and in August 1864 an advertisement described him as 'late a prisoner for debt.' This business decline probably explains Woodley's approach to Brunel for his possible purchase of Great Burradon, five and a half acres of prime land facing southwards towards Torbay.

From Brunel's reply it seems likely that Woodley had tried to 'talk up' the value of his land by suggesting that he might sell it as a building-site, a proposal crisply dismissed by Brunel in his letter of 22nd October 1857 – just eleven days before the launch of *Great Eastern*. 'My dear, Sir,

You and I need not try to agree as to the eligibility of your field for a building site – there is no doubt that it is a very airy situation commanding a fine view – and if you can make more of it by building than by selling it to me you would be most unwise not to do so. Neither need we discuss its value – the value to you is what you can make of it – of this I know nothing, its value to me is what I am willing to give for it, and that is all I know. I was once willing to give more than I am now – but even now

assuming it to contain five and a half acres and that the boundaries are what I believe them to be (but I have no plans here in town) and that it extends up to the common from the end of my walk by your summer-house to the corner of the field beyond. I will give you a thousand pounds – if this offer is accepted at once – I must not let this opportunity pass without reminding you that you have not yet moved the post and rails which you set too far into my road. I really must have this done. I hope to be down at Christmas – and must do it myself if you have not, but as a gentleman, you ought not to leave me to such a remedy.

Yours truly,

I.K. Brunel'

A 'bird in the hand' must have been overwhelmingly tempting to Woodley, for Brunel sent a further letter two days later: 'It is very difficult for me to make appointments but I am almost always at home [Duke Street] in the morning from 9 till 1030 – and in the evenings after 8.30 – but in the evenings I generally have engagements. I have no plans whatever of the Marychurch property in London.' (This letter provides further evidence that Brunel was not overwhelmed by the launching problem and spending morning, noon and night down at Millwall.)

These two letters to Woodley, together with other supporting evidence, indicate that Brunel was as resolved as ever to pursue his Watcombe Adventure. They are not the letters of a man driven out of

Floating the first Tube of the Royal Albert Bridge at Saltash in 1857

Further evidence of Brunel's well-being at this stage of his life is provided by John Horsley's portrait – one of the few of which the provenance is absolutely certain. It is dated 1857 by the artist, and was exhibited in the Royal Academy Exhibition which was held from 4th May until 25th July that year. The iconic study of Brunel is Robert Howlett's photograph, taken before the launching chains of the *Great Eastern*, with cigar in mouth, baggy trousers and Thames mud on his boots. This vision of Brunel has come to symbolise the heroism of industrial Britain. Horsley's image is of Brunel as country gentleman, seated at his desk – planning perhaps the planting of trees rather than the construction of ships. This portrait by Brunel's brother-in- law may not be a 'warts and all' likeness, but the contrast with the photographs taken on the *Great Eastern* just two years later is startling. This is

his mind by worry. In particular that first letter with its detail, its carefully turned phrases, its firm reproof to Woodley that he ought to behave like a gentleman – show that the *Great Eastern* was not 'all-consuming', that Watcombe and its future was still a leading element in Brunel's life. His son Isambard endorsed this view in the *Life* of his father published in 1870, stating that many visits were paid to Watcombe in 1857. (It was in September 1857 that Brunel scored his most spectacular success. It was then that he 'stage-managed' the floating of the first section of the Saltash Bridge.) Isambard stressed that this was an especially happy time for the family, and especially for Brunel himself. 'There can be little doubt that the happiest hours of his life were spent in walking about in the gardens with his wife and children, and discussing the condition and prospect of his favourite trees.'

Florence Brunel. Anonymous.

Isambard Brunel 1837 - 1902, the Brunel's eldest son, in his legal robes. Anonymous.

John Horsley's 1857 Portrait of Brunel Credit: Isambard Kingdom Brunel (1806-59) (oil on canvas) by Horsley, John Callcott (1817-1903) © Bristol City Museum and Art Gallery, UK/ The Bridgeman Art Library

clearly not a man ground down by illness and racked by worry and overwork. It is the picture of a man at ease with himself and with the world: of a man poised to write calmly to Woodley about those five and a half acres of land, even when beset with the launch of his Great Ship.

'…the improvement of this property was his chief delight…'

From these various clues it seems probable that Brunel became more deeply involved in Watcombe than his biographers – even his son Isambard – ever appreciated. To Rolt 'the luxury and order of Duke Street…was the one stable thing in his restless, hectic life,'

but possibly Watcombe contributed at a deeper level to a sense of continuity and of enduring values at a time of rapid change. It was Brunel's own creation, discovered by him, planned by him, financed by him. Here was an enterprise that required no Act of Parliament, no uncertain allies, no scramble to attract outside investors. Much has been made of Brunel's investment of money and reputation in *Great Eastern*: but his investment in Watcombe was also substantial. Over the past years he had spent at least £23,000 on purchasing and developing the estate; but over and above this was the sustained emotional involvement. Once again his son's biography, despite its approach of clinical detachment, provides some clues. 'The improvement of this property was his chief delight.' The arrangement of his plantations 'gave him unfailing pleasure.' Here was an enterprise in which all the

Sir Marc Brunel, pictured here writing left handed, following his stroke. Anonymous.

The Young Gardener's Assistant commended flower gardening as 'a delightful employment, and well adapted to the amusement of a lady...' Both at Watcombe, and subsequently at Froude's 'Chelston Cross', Mary Brunel's contribution was significant.

As for Brunel himself, his enthusiasm is recorded in that Watcombe Garden Book – above all in his comment about planting Mountain Ash: 'everywhere that I can stick them for the sake of the

family could share. Before his death late in 1849 old Sir Marc was pushed round the new estate roads in a bath chair, falling in love with the blue convolvulus which was later sent up to his sick-room in London. Watcombe became a family enterprise, and it seems likely that Mary Brunel played a major part in the outcome. There are references in the Garden Book to her suggestions; and there is the naming of 'Mary's Clump' which may indicate that she planned its layout. Above all there is the testimony of her future son-in-law that 'the grounds were laid out by her.' By now gardening had become not only acceptable but strongly recommended as an occupation for ladies. In 1845 Louisa Johnson's *Every Lady her own Flower Gardener* wrote that 'the amusement of floriculture has become the dominant passion of the ladies of Great Britain.' Two years later Thomas Bridgeman's

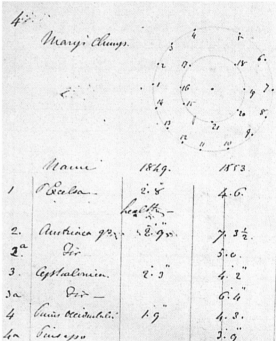

Mary's clump from Brunels Garden Book.
© University of Bristol

Blue Convolvulus

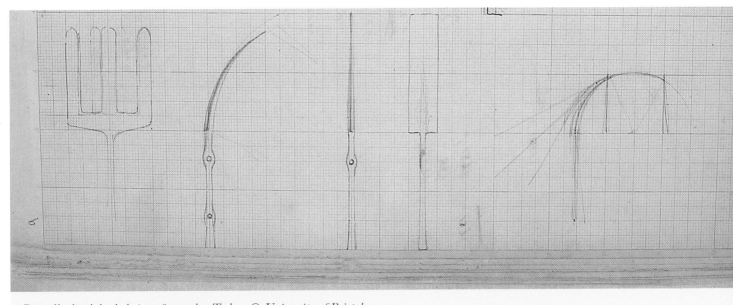

Brunel's sketch book designs for garden Tools © *University of Bristol*

berries e.g. 200.' This enthusiasm found expression in so many details of his estate – his carefully constructed avenues, the timber bridge he planned across the turnpike road, his specially designed tools for moving large trees. Brunel's ingenuity perhaps lay behind the device, described by his gardener Forsyth, for ensuring the vertical planting of trees on sloping ground: certainly he designed special labels for his specimen trees. Six pages of the Garden Book are taken up by detailed measurements of these trees between 1849 and 1856, along with comments upon their condition. Most of these trees were between 2' and 4' when first measured, though some planted in the Lower Ground were as large as 8'. Two further pages contain detailed drawings of some particular trees – for example an Araucaria in the Lower Garden was sketched with some of its measurements on August 31st 1853. Rolt attributed the paucity of measurements beyond 1855 as evidence of a slackening interest, but there may well be other explanations. By 1855 most of the trees were recorded as healthy – only a few are described as 'dead' or 'very shabby', 'struggling' or 'cut down and just living': and on several of these pages the final measurements are crammed against the right-hand margin – to have continued recording for subsequent years would have involved the inconvenience of copying out in larger format, or of starting fresh columns on later pages.

Lack of measurement does not imply lack of concern. With most trees well-established, a continuing solicitude was probably no longer appropriate. Equally likely Brunel had discovered that down here in Devon he no longer needed to surround his life at every waking moment with exact dimensions: quality rather than quantity was to be his secret. A revealing incident in the life of his son Henry may provide a clue. In 1880 Henry joined his brother on a trip to Normandy to learn more about his ancestors at the

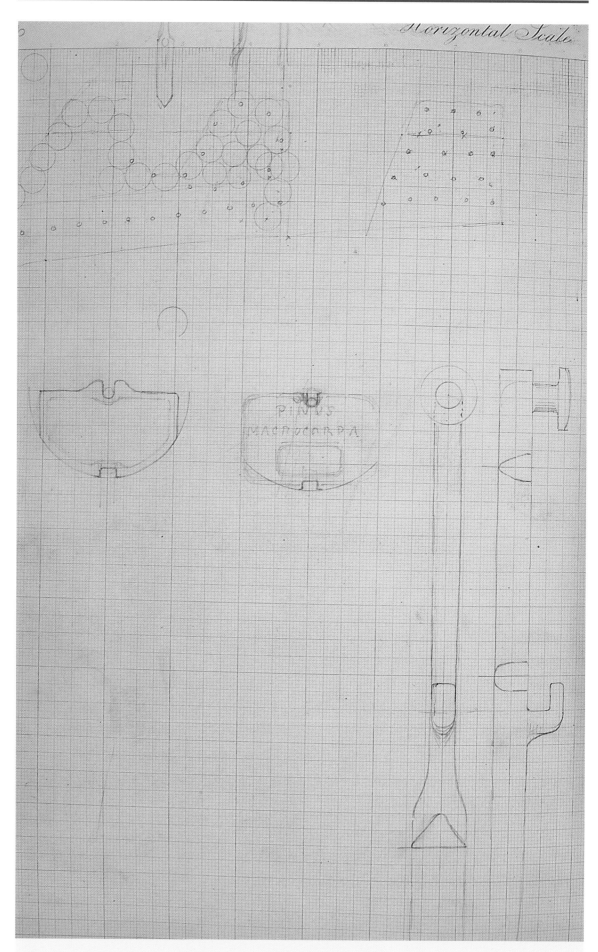

Tree Plaque Designs from Brunel's sketch books © *University of Bristol*

Brunel's recipe for a winter dressing for his specimen trees © *University of Bristol*

'Ferme Brunel'. His grandfather, Marc Brunel, had begun his life there, but Henry – with his prejudices and his 'rusty' French – was now a thorough Englishman. He described this French expedition in a whimsical letter to his friend, Eddy Froude. Other members of the family, he wrote, 'had the good sense to stay rooted in the good French earth at Hacqueville, to live quietly and not trouble themselves with such things as meters, logs, boats and the like.'

> 'Happy the man whose wish
> and care
> A few paternal acres bound,
> Content to breathe his native air,
> In his own ground.'

Like the man described by Pope, Brunel's mind may have been beguiled and his personality mellowed through his Watcombe Adventure. It is well worth considering, not only how Brunel altered Watcombe, but also how Watcombe may have altered him.

When planning his planting programme in 1855 (October 15th) Brunel must have mislaid his notebook – perhaps he left it in London in August after noting the measurements of his trees. His 'Rough Memo for planting this autumn' is written on a large loose sheet folded to provide four pages: fortunately it was later placed inside the Garden Book and has remained safely there over the years. (That same month – October 1855 – Brunel began a series of 'Memoranda for my Own Guidance' where he jotted down any bright ideas for the *Great Eastern* - for example a railway let into the deck 'along which a truck can carry dinner etc. etc. from the Kitchen to each saloon.' Watcombe planning and Great Ship planning were moving forward concurrently.)

In the 'Watcombe Rough Memo.' of 1855 there appears for the first time a concern with providing contrasting colour – '2 or 3 yews in front of ashes – two or three maples and oaks and other plants which have autumnal tints.' Behind the ashes would be placed 'two insignis to create a dark background.' There is a growing sense of profusion – as with the scattering of Mountain Ash 'wherever I can stick them for the sake of the berries.' Now it was Berberis that was to be planted under the Arbutus and 'in front of beds everywhere.' (2,000 Berberis plants were specified!) Cotoneaster was to be thickened around the Arucaria plantation and planted 'plentifully' on the bank of the Summer-house. Fifty Luccombe Oak – a Devon speciality – were to be planted at the south end of the drive to correspond with those to the north. Beds of gorse should be placed under the Wood Walk above the quarry: 'have all the gorse clipped.' The thorn plantation was to be reinforced by transplanting 'any larger old ones to be found by the hedge.' Brunel was involving himself in detail now: 'Yew – plant 3 above Wood Walk, just above the top of zig-zag.' (It was almost like a general planning the disposition of his troops.) Five places are listed where patches of ivy should be planted and then comes the detail for providing a winter dressing for some of the specimen trees. 'To prepare and apply a plentiful supply of vegetable mould, wood ash and bone with just a little Guano and soda and burnt clay and apply to all the chosen trees...' (Guano – concentrated sea-bird droppings from Peru and other places – had first arrived around 1841 and was by now

very much the 'in thing': growers had discovered how to use it in judicious quantities. It was a telling sign that in 1853 The *Agricultural Gazette* observed that 'the old yeoman now likes guano.') The Japanese Red Cedar was specified for special treatment, along with 'the small old oak at bottom of home garden': clearly that tree must have needed a boost.

Apart from a few jottings on the pages recording tree measurements, there are no details given for the years 1856 and 1857. It has been noted that Brunel was frequently at Watcombe in 1857, so all planning may have been done verbally. In addition there had been a staff change. By now there was a new head gardener, Alexander Forsyth having returned north in 1856 to manage a corn-mill. His successor was Willliam Elston, who later moved into 'Hacqueville', the Brunel property in St. Marychurch. He was recorded as living at 'Hacqueville' in the earliest parish rate-book in 1867. Elston seems to have stayed on for some time after Brunel's death, maintaining the grounds until the property was sold. His name appears quite frequently in Henry Brunel's letters, and he was called upon – along with Mary Brunel – to assist with the laying out of William Froude's grounds at 'Chelston Cross'. By 1871 Elston had moved away to Somerset to trade as an ironmonger: as with Forsyth, increasing age and aching limbs may have indicated the need for a less strenuous profession.

CHAPTER 8:
The End of Brunel's Watcombe Adventure

At work in the gardens, Easter 1858

In the spring of 1858, with *Great Eastern* safely launched, Brunel could once again turn his attention to Watcombe. His health must have been greatly shattered by all the trials of the launch, as shown by the kindly invitation received early in February from Mr Hill of Plymouth Iron Works, South Wales. 'Your mind must want the relief of a little rest: cannot you cut anxiety, for a short time, and come here, to spend a week quietly with me: you shall [have] a comfortable warm bedroom (this snowy weather)…' Not much later we find Brunel gardening with his wife in Devon: probably he felt that the relaxed pace and gentle challenge of Watcombe provided the best rest-cure. Woodley's land was purchased, and substantial sums were sent down to the Torquay bankers between February and May to finance the long-delayed construction of the house.

From another source, early in 1858, comes a fascinating glimpse of that brief period at Watcombe when it seems to have been 'full steam ahead'. Staying nearby that Easter was young Arthur James, then a schoolboy at Eton. (In future years he was to marry

Florence Brunel grew up to marry Eton Master. Arthur James. Their daughter Celia perpetuated the lineage, if not the name, of Brunel. Neither of Brunel's sons had children. Anonymous.

Brunel's daughter, Florence, who gave birth to a daughter, Celia, to perpetuate the lineage, if not the name, of Brunel.) Many years later Arthur James, by then a house-master at Eton, recorded this visit to Watcombe and his first impression of the Brunels. 'While at Watcombe I went with the party over to visit the Brunels. . . Mr. Brunel, whom I saw for the first and only time, I remember as a little business-looking man in seedy dress and with a foot-rule in his hand. Mrs Brunel was planning and setting out gardens, where

Brunel's Grand daughter, Celia, married Sir William Armstrong Noble 3rd Bt. Through their children, the lineage of Isambard Kingdom Brunel continues today.   Anonymous

'Watcombe House' was afterwards situated. The grounds were laid out by her, but Mr. Brunel died and the property was sold before the house was built.' By now *Great Eastern* was safely launched, and it was red Devon clay and not Thames mud that Brunel had on his boots. This picture of Brunel clad in his old gardening clothes is an endearing one – as is the thought that Mary Brunel could literally 'get down to earth' as well as saunter in St. James Park or glitter in the ballroom. Such gardening activities were soon to be interrupted by a serious breakdown in Brunel's health: his doctors advised residence abroad and he was out of the country in Italy and Switzerland from May to September. This could account for the fact that the 'planting notes' for 1858 took place in October rather than in August as in earlier years.

There is a problem in dating here, because Brunel's scrawl is more than usually illegible when it came to recording dates. The entry on page 21 of the notebook begins with a jotting in pencil: 'M. to plant trees to supplant old bed which now below wood walk above new Berberis.' Then comes a date: this appears to be October 5 / 58, though that last figure might equally well be a 6. There is internal evidence, however, to suggest that the date was 1858 rather than 1856:
1) A reference appears to 'Portland Villa', the house to which the Brunels moved in the spring of 1857.
2) Black spruce was to be planted 'on brow of new hill' – probably a reference to the land just purchased from Woodley - the 'airy site commanding a fine view.'
3) The new hill would also provide the setting for a formidable grove of Araucaria: 100 young ones would be placed there or 'to be transplanting our own.' It seems unlikely that home-grown stock would be available in such quantities for transplanting before 1858.
4) Luccombe Oak was to be purchased 'for carriage drive and other places.' This would seem to refer to Brunel's approach drive down from Great Hill, a project that was not fully completed at his death.
5) Most of the suggestions seem to be of an 'afterthought' nature, designed to rectify mistakes or supplement work carried out earlier. There is reference for the first time to a Summerhouse Walk: there followed a suggestion to provide a 'necklace of old ivy roots, wattle, stones and other such things for ivy to grow in over the grass.'

Brunel's illness and death

Apart from a few jottings, some in pencil, which are difficult to date, this appears to be the end of Brunel's garden planning. On 1st September 1858 the *Torquay Directory* had announced: 'We have great pleasure in stating that I.K. Brunel Esq., the celebrated engineer, has returned to his residence, 'Portland Villa' near this town, with restored health.' This apparent restoration would have allowed the final instalment of garden planning, but the paper's optimism was premature: this was no more than a brief respite. Very shortly there came the grim diagnosis of Bright's disease and the December departure for Egypt. Signs appear of Brunel, knowing he was doomed, beginning to draw a line under his Watcombe Adventure. Early in December he successfully wound up the Watson affair, but there was also a land issue to be settled. The wealthy tea merchant, James Peek, had bought the former Brunel residence, 'Watcombe Villa'. (Villas were now two a penny in the area, so the property was soon given the grander-sounding name of 'Watcombe Lodge'.) The Peeks intended to build a chapel on what came to be known later as 'Mrs Peek's Teafield' and access was needed over Brunel's land. On 6th December 1858 Brunel sent Peek a letter on the issue. 'I thought it was as an access to your land that you wanted the Road and I intended therefore to tell you to use it for the present and that I should be ready to make some arrangement to give you the right of user

but I could not sell it, as it could materially affect the value of my other property as an access to it should it come to be sold in parts.' For the first time a note of uncertainty about the future enters one of Brunel's letters about Watcombe. By now he must have realised that his dream was nearing its end, and that he would need to sell the estate to provide for his family's future.

Although a sick man Brunel continued to live life to the lees: in a Mediterranean storm he wedged himself on deck to take observations of wind and wave; at Christmas he dined with Robert Stephenson in Cairo; in February he combined the excitement of a schoolboy and the professionalism of an engineer as thirty-five labourers hauled their boat through the Nile cataracts above Aswan. 'Until I had seen it and calculated the power required I should imprudently have said it could not be effected... getting under the boat to push it off the rocks, all with an immense expenditure of noise, apparent confusion and want of plan – yet, on the whole, properly and successfully.' Returning via Rome, Brunel was back in London in mid-May, ready for the final heave to get *Great Eastern* to sea. Not only were many technical matters to be resolved, there was also the raising of additional funds to prepare for the sea-trials. In Rolt's opinion, '...by this time he was very well aware that his disease was mortal and that even if he allowed himself to become a complete invalid the end could not long be postponed. A man of his spirit scorned to take any lease of life on such terms as that.' The ship must come first and the Watcombe dream must be abandoned. On 18th June 1859 Brunel wrote to Mr. Hamlyn: 'You will receive this as notice of my intention to terminate the lease of the house at Maiden Combe ['Portland Villa'] at Christmas.'

Long before Christmas, on 15th September, Brunel was dead: the only subsequent letter in the Brunel papers about Watcombe came from Secretary Joseph Bennett on 26th December,

Brunel's final touch. A letter from Joseph Bennett was sent to Dawson. 'Before the plan can be lithographed, Mr. Brunel wishes to go through it carefully – as he finds that in parts it is far from accurate according to his recollection.' ©University of Bristol

dealing with the insurance of the various properties pending decisions on their future. Brunel's own final involvement was in checking the details of the Watcombe Estate map drawn up by William Dawson during the summer. This fascinating map provides firm evidence of Brunel's achievement as estate builder and landscaper. It shows the 136 acres accumulated in a series of purchases over the years – along with that inconvenient Codner's Piece that he had been unable to grasp. It shows that many roads and paths had been constructed, and thousands of trees planted, to create an extensive designed landscape. It also shows, bleakly, 'site of house, altitude 500 feet,' marking the foundations and the garden terraces already completed. Just a year earlier young Arthur James had seen Brunel and his wife at work laying out those gardens: now all was over. But not quite over! Time still remained for Brunel's final touch. A letter from Joseph Bennett was sent to Dawson. 'Before the plan can be lithographed, Mr. Brunel wishes to go through it carefully – as he finds that in parts it is far from accurate according to his recollection.' He must have paced every quarter of his Watcombe estate: every part of it must have been imprinted on his memory.

'...admitting any person to view the grounds.'

It is important to stress that Brunel's burgeoning wonderland was not to flourish for the enjoyment of family and friends alone. His gardener was instructed 'to have the liberty of admitting any person to view the grounds' – a handsome approach to his property rights that was far from general at the time. 'Cockington', at the opposite end of Torquay, provides an example of a much less generous approach: there the Mallocks retained lakes and landscaped grounds strictly for their own enjoyment – as a cause celebre of the time demonstrated. A local gentleman appears to have won such favour with the Mallocks that he was invited to make himself free of the grounds, along with his friends, at any time. Taking up this invitation, he was wandering in the woods with his party of friends when they were accosted by one of Mallock's keepers, who proceeded to turn them away. One of the gentlemen in the party, judging the keeper's language not sufficiently choice in the presence of ladies, struck him to the ground. The keeper took the man to court for assault and won his case: the gentleman was found guilty and fined.

The most interesting aspect of the affair was not the affray itself, but the attitudes revealed in the resulting correspondence in the local press - which rumbled on for weeks. Lord Chesterfield had stated that, on being offended, there were only two paths open to a gentleman – extreme politeness or knocking down: many correspondents suggested that this was not a suitable case for extreme politeness and that 'knocking down' was the only course open to a gentleman.

Others wrote to the paper on the 'right to roam' aspect of the affair: a man fortunate enough to own such a paradise as 'Cockington' should not display the 'dog-in-the-mangerish' attitude of keeping its pleasures all to himself. This was an attitude with which Brunel would have heartily agreed. (So would Augustus Smith, hero of the Berkhamsted Common battleground. When he came to lay out his famous sub-tropical garden at Tresco Abbey he practised what he had preached. An inscribed slate tablet still proclaims that 'all islanders are welcome to walk in these gardens.' Visitors are requested [not ordered!] to keep to the main walks, not to pick flowers or fruit, and to abstain from 'scribbling nonsense.' Subject to these mild restraints: 'Enter then, if it please you, and welcome.' One feels that Brunel and Augustus Smith – both forceful characters – would have enjoyed each other's company.)

'...the dream of a peaceful retirement to the West Country'?

Brunel was a man who knew where he was going – though sometimes unsure of how he would get there. In developing his home and park at Watcombe he must have possessed some concept of the form of life he would follow there, had he survived to the allotted span of three score years and ten. Rolt's biography stressed the dramatic tension of the *Great Eastern* saga: in his words: 'Brunel's last enterprise had become all-consuming

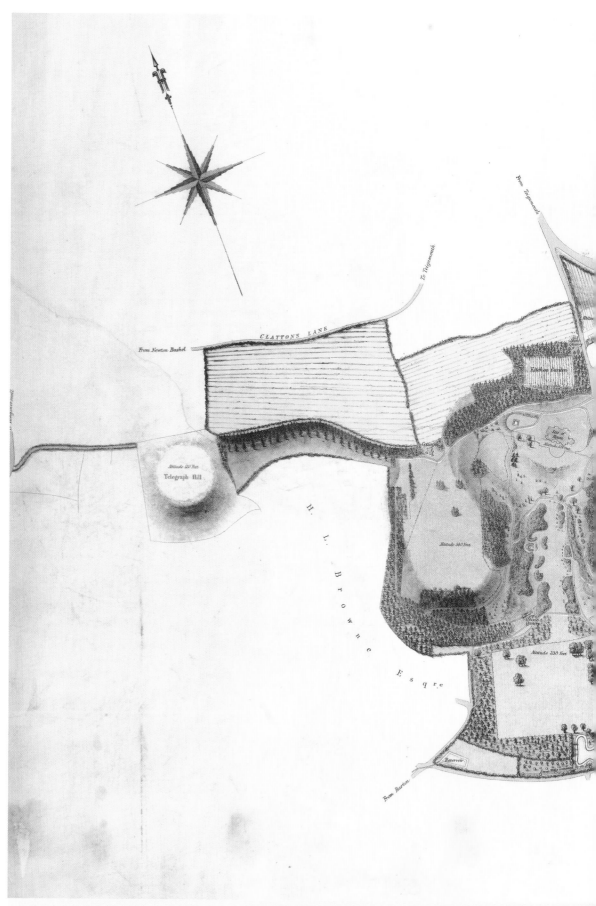

Brunel's own final involvement was in checking the details of the Watcombe Estate map drawn up by William Dawson during the summer of 1859. This fascinating map provides firm evidence of Brunel's achievement as estate builder and landscaper. It shows the 136 acres accumulated in a series of purchases over the years © *Devon Record Office*

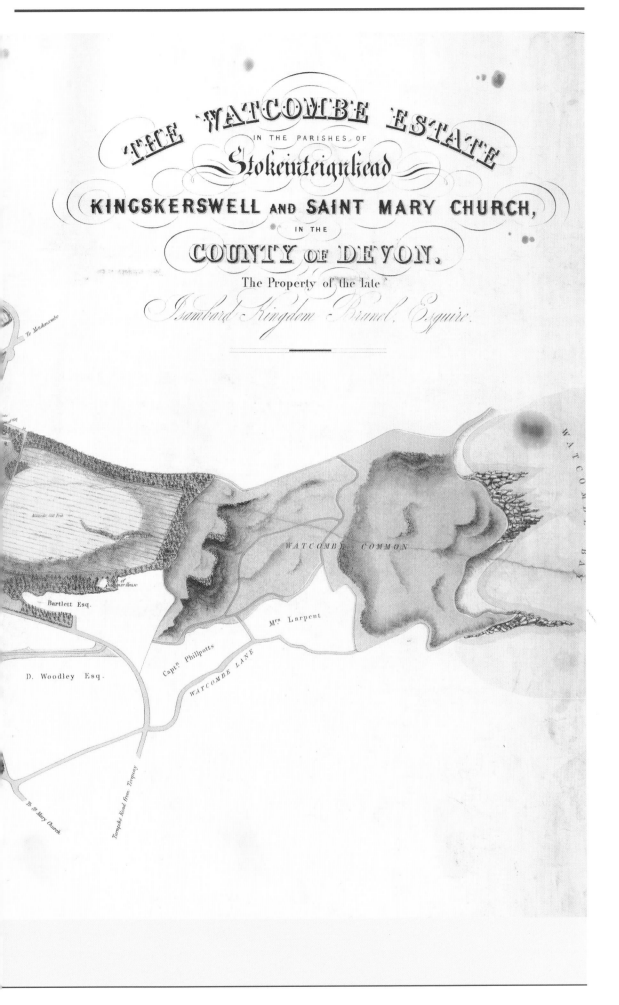

THE WATCOMBE ESTATE

IN THE PARISHES OF

Stokeinteignhead

KINGSKERSWELL AND SAINT MARY CHURCH,

IN THE

COUNTY OF DEVON.

The Property of the late

Isambard Kingdom Brunel, Esquire.

To Maidencombe

Altitude 600 Feet

WATCOMBE BAY

WATCOMBE COMMON

Site of Summer House

Bartlett Esq.

Mrs Larpent

Captn Phillpotts

WATCOMBE LANE

D. Woodley Esq.

Turnpike Road from Torquay

To St Mary Church

and the dream of a peaceful retirement to the West Country was driven ever further into the background of his thoughts.' But it seems most improbable that a man of Brunel's temperament would have buried himself away in peaceful retirement. Such a concept clashed with Rolt's own insight in his Preface: 'The further I went the clearer did it seem to me that, large though the achievement was, the man was larger still. Brunel, in fact, was more than a great engineer; he was an artist and a visionary.'

The plan for the intended house at Watcombe provides us with a clue, for a large workshop was included – not tucked away in some back corner but in a central position next to the study. Brunel had developed his manual skills in Breguet's workshop and was an accomplished model-maker, but that workshop might well have had wider purposes. It has not been sufficiently stressed that Brunel was a researcher as well as a constructor. Not only much of his own time, but also that of assistants such as William Bell at Bristol, was spent in assessing the properties of various materials and the strengths of different constructional forms. His Great Ship was in part conceived as a floating research station. Performance was to be carefully recorded and evaluated with the aid of new measuring devices – a point stressed by William Froude in an address to the Institution of Naval Architects in 1861. In his paper on *The Rolling of Ships*, he remarked that it resulted from an enquiry undertaken at the request of the late Mr. Brunel; and he acknowledged that he had received 'the greatest assistance from his broad and masculine perceptions.'

At 'Chelston Cross' a vast semi-basement extending below the frontage of the house provided space for the researchers and their projects. This was 'serviced' by adjacent forge, metal workshop and carpenters' shop. Most of the equipment needed by the research station was produced on-site. Image: Peter Lemar

It seems certain that Brunel would have become deeply involved with his friend William Froude in tackling the three main problems presented by the steamship – hull shape, efficient propulsion and stability. In the event it was Brunel's son Henry who joined with Froude in developing 'Chelston Cross' at Torquay into both home and research station. How Brunel would have envied its facilities, extending far beyond the simple workshop he had envisaged at Watcombe! At 'Chelston Cross' a vast semi-basement extending below the frontage of the house provided space for the researchers and their projects. This was 'serviced' by adjacent forge, metal workshop and carpenters' shop. Most of the equipment needed by the research station was produced on-site. William Froude had a reputation as a superb craftsman. The famous Oxford doctor, Sir Henry Acland, said of him: 'No workman in any art ever combined in juster proportions, few in so eminent degree, the three properties of culture, science and practice. His hands were as skilful as his creative brain was active.' This was state-of-the-art research carried out on a shoestring. (Henry Brunel solved one of their supply problems – the lack of squared paper of sufficient accuracy to meet their high standards. At the cost of £57 29s he devised *Mr Brunel's Paper-Ruling Machine*. Until the 1970's it continued to supply all the squared paper required by the Admiralty Research Establishment at Haslar. For cost-effectiveness that must be some kind of record.)

Many of the design features at 'Chelston Cross' came, not from the architect – who was sacked - but from Henry Brunel (21) and Froude's son Eddy (17). Here the world's first effective experiments were conducted to relate the performance of models in a tank to that of full-sized ships at sea. Between 1870 and 1886 the research centre was given government support as the Admiralty Experiment Works, becoming the setting for 97 different trials - the results of these forming the basis of the modern science of ship dynamics. The break-through came in December 1871 when Henry wrote to his brother

The World's first marine testing tank, disguised as a chapel building at Chelston Cross, the home of William Froude, where Henry Brunel lodged and participated in experiments to test the performance of model ships
Image: Peter Lemar

Isambard to describe one of the outstanding moments in maritime research: 'They tried their first real experiment in the tank on Saturday, towing a model of the *Greyhound* with great success, the results agreeing with the full-size experiment.' (Had I.K. Brunel lived to 65 he could have shared this moment: and Henry might have added, when writing to his brother Isambard, 'Papa was delighted!')

Work on ships was central to the research at 'Chelston Cross', but the group of brilliant and inventive men who worked there formed a 'think-tank' at the cutting edge of technology. There was William Metford of projectile fame; Beauchamp Tower, creator of the spherical engine and researcher in high-pressure lubrication; Arnulph Mallock, pioneer in optical measurement. (One of his devices could detect a crack of a millionth of an inch in the fabric of St. Paul's Cathedral caused by the vibration from underground trains: Mallock lived long enough - until 1933 - to become one of the country's first 'boffins' during the Great War.)

In 1873 they were joined by young Frank Purvis, who later built the Denny Ship Tank at Dumbarton, moving on to become Professor of Naval Architecture at Tokyo. How Brunel would have revelled in the company of such men! And how richly he might have contributed to their scheming!

Living at Watcombe among his burgeoning trees, sharing in Froude's experiments while no longer a 'slave' to the toil, Brunel might perhaps have won through to the personal fulfilment that had so long eluded him. This band of researchers at 'Chelston Cross' resembled the mariners in Tennyson's *Ulysses*:

'Souls that have toil'd, and wrought, and thought with me –'

These men were winning the mastery over the sea's challenges that Brunel had sought, and their triumphs would have given him both pride and comfort.

Grounds Right Slope 1903 © *National Monumental Record*

CHAPTER 9:
The Brunel Family and Torquay

Henry Brunel's 'Great Bridge at Watcombe.'

Brunel died at his London home on 15th September, 1859. He was found to have left about £90,000 – less than the fortunes built up by other leading engineers of his day. Sorting out his financial affairs, with so many engineering enterprises in being, was a complex and lengthy task: to a considerable extent the future of Watcombe was linked to the future of the Great Ship Company. For four years the Watcombe property remained in family hands. Though first offered for sale in December 1859 it was subsequently withdrawn: not until January 1863 did a sale notice reappear. There are frequent references in Henry Brunel's letters to various aspects of estate maintenance and winding down. One piece of unfinished business was the erection of the timber bridge leading across the Teignmouth Road to Brunel's Sea Walks. Henry seems to have looked upon this task as a matter of honour – much as the Institution of Civil Engineers regarded the unfinished Clifton Bridge as 'a slur upon the engineering talent of the country.'

The project probably had its origin as far back as 1857, when Henry Brunel,

aged fifteen, was granted three months leave of absence from Harrow. The object was to obtain what we would now call 'work experience' on some of his father's projects; and one such project was what Henry somewhat grandiloquently termed 'The Great Bridge at Maidencombe'. (The earliest drawing in Henry's Sketchbook is entitled: 'Exaggerated drawing of a pole for a new bridge over the road at Maidencombe.' This 'new' bridge would evidently replace the temporary construction shown on the

This photograph of Henry Brunel's Great bridge over the Teignmouth road at Watcombe was taken on the 16th February 1891

1859 estate map.) Detailed drawings must have been prepared, and the required timber assembled and placed in pickling tanks at Bridgwater sawmills. In December 1860 Henry wrote to a friend: 'I do not know if I shall go to Paignton this Christmas, but if I do I shall finish the great bridge.' (Seemingly whether he could go or not depended upon the 'excommunication' of black beetles from William Froude's Paignton home – a large drawing of one decorates Henry's letter.)

The beetles must have been worsted, because Henry came to stay and the project was set in motion. It took much longer than Henry in his youthful optimism had predicted. Letters and telegrams flew back and forth over several months, and kindly Mr. Froude made several visits to the site to ensure that the work was completed to a high standard. Thirty gallons of creosote added further protection to the 'pickled' timber, and the bridge certainly endured. How long it lasted remains uncertain. One photograph was taken on the 16th February 1891, and there are two picture postcards dating from the early 1900's. The bridge certainly outlasted Henry, who died on 7th November 1903, being mentioned in local guidebooks after that date, though no record has been traced for its disappearance.
It must have been dismantled, for a local gardener, J. Moyse, recorded how he came upon a puzzled group of soldiers on a map-reading exercise. They were earnestly seeking a bridge that was marked on their map, but which they could not discover. He reassured them that their map-reading was not at fault; it was a rustic bridge that had fallen into disrepair, had become dangerous, and had been removed.

Henry's bridge lasted, then, for around fifty years – about as long as some of his father's timber railway bridges. It won widespread attention and may possibly have been copied in other locations. In 1873 a Mr. C.O. Burdon requested details and Henry found that the original drawings had been mislaid. He wrote at once to Watcombe, seeking permission to enter the estate. 'Will you give me leave to take some photographs of the bridge over the road? I have been asked to give a drawing of it and I think photographs may turn out to be the best way of giving an idea of it,' Subsequent correspondence indicates that measurements were taken as well as photographs, and that plans were drawn up and a model constructed. (Perhaps they may still be held by some heir of that Mr. Burdon whose enquiry spurred Henry to so much activity.)

Watcombe's emotional grip

With the estate remaining in family hands for four years following Brunel's death, there was plenty of coming and going around the area. Henry Brunel had spent Christmas 1861 at Paignton, among thoughts of beetles and bridges. Christmas 1862 was spent in a villa called 'The Marina' rented by Mrs

Brunel at the top of the steep lane dropping down to Maidencombe. Henry was there for ten days, travelling down from his apprenticeship with Sir William Armstrong at Newcastle. As usual there were elaborate family theatricals, with performances both for family guests and for the local population, estate workers and servants. (Metford, the explosives expert, was called upon to provide lighting and 'effects' to Mary Brunel's alarm.) All too quickly it was time for Henry to return to his dreary life at Newcastle: but his Letterbooks show what a continuing hold Watcombe exercised not only on the Brunel family, but also on their servants. In May 1879, nearly twenty years after Brunel's death, Henry wrote to the new owner, Colonel Wright, seeking permission for a visit to the gardens by the former gardener's wife and by Henry's 'Nurse', Mrs Egan.

1879 was also the year when Henry was appointed Consulting Engineer to Torquay's Waterworks Committee, thus 'firming up' a role which he had been performing off and on for the last thirteen years. At times he was close to resigning after being thoroughly messed around by 'butchers and bakers…who think themselves competent to decide on anything.' (They had backed out of providing Henry with the stream gauge and rain gauge required to calculate how quickly his reservoir would fill.) But now in 1879 the 'retired butchers, masons and china dealers' were thrown out by the 'revolutionary' party, and a doctor and two other 'gentlefolk' elected to

Torquay's Board of Health to Henry's delight. (Like his father he had a powerful belief in the standards of the 'gentleman.') By 1885 a new reservoir had been constructed and filled at Hennick, and the threat of water-rationing during drought summers had been removed. The Brunel family's involvement in Torquay continued, in one way and another, for nearly thirty years after I.K. Brunel's death in 1859.

Purchasers for Watcombe Park

Apart from the complexities of Brunel's estate, there must have been difficulties in disposing of a property well-endowed with young woodland but with no house. The estate was eventually purchased by two brothers Vicary, tanners from Newton Abbot, who must have bought it as a speculation. (Henry Brunel told his mother it had been sold much too cheaply – sparking off one of their many family rows.) It was still apparently in Vicary hands when a party came to visit from the British Association gathering in Exeter. The occasion was reported by the *Torquay Directory* on 8th September, 1869.

'After visiting the Echo Rock at Watcombe… the party proceeded to the beautiful grounds owned by Mr. Vicary, who met them on the spot where the late Mr. Brunel constructed the ground-plan of his intended mansion. After the usual courtesies the party were put in charge of Mr. Elton [should read Elston] the head-gardener, who spared no pains in pointing out the magnificent groves of

Pinus Insignis, the large Wellingtonias and Piceas, the Taxodiums, Deodaras, Cryptomerias, and all the other interesting varieties of conifers which flourish here in luxuriance and beauty…The party were in excellent spirits, and much amusement was caused by the ineffectual attempts of some of the ladies to climb the smooth slopes of closely mown-turf , which the dry weather had rendered as slippery as a glacier. At the lower end of the grounds they were met by Mr. Vicary, who had prepared for them a sumptuous luncheon, with champagne and other choice wines, in a building sheltered from the rays of the sun.'

From this account it would seem that there was less decorum and more high jinks than might have been expected in such an august Victorian assembly! The luncheon must have taken place on or near the site where sixteen years earlier Mrs Brunel had entertained the children to tea and buns, and their elders to roast beef and plum pudding. (Mr. Vicary was perhaps hoping to discover a purchaser as a result of this invitation and lavish entertainment.)

One way or another, a purchaser was found - James Roper Crompton, a wealthy paper manufacturer from Lancashire. Crompton built most of the present house and stables. In 1876 it was sold on to Colonel Charles Ichabod Wright, from an old-established Nottingham banking family. He had moved from Sussex to Stapleford Hall, Nottinghamshire, on the death of his father in 1871. There he greatly extended his garden and planted many of the new conifers. (Being Colonel of the Robin Hood Rifles he had hit upon an unusual method of pruning unwanted leading shoots by knocking them off with rifle shots.) Insufficient scope for extending his plantations may well have persuaded him to purchase Brunel's splendid arboretum.

Colonel Wright now had time on his hands. For just over a year he had held a seat in Parliament, but it seems he had 'a dislike of the stormy atmosphere of political life.' A book on *Great Houses and County Families of Nottinghamshire*, (1881) described Colonel Wright as a 'high-minded English gentleman who divides his time between Stapleford Hall and Watcombe Park, between Nottinghamshire and Devonshire.' Watcombe must have provided a comfortable winter retreat in the mild climate of Torbay. During the summer there was the continuing oversight of suburban development on Wright family lands in Carrington and Mapperley. Both school and church at Carrington had been financed largely by the Wrights: finally, in 1886 a vicarage was added, sited at the corner of Watcombe Circus and Watcombe Road. (The names brought a touch of Devon north to Nottinghamshire.)

Down in Devon, at a cost of £22,900, Colonel Wright had obtained the main house – now called 'Watcombe Park' –

along with large stable-block, several workers dwellings and cottages. That would appear to be something of a bargain when all Brunel's extensive plantings are taken into account. It was now seventeen years after his death, but Mary Brunel had retained an emotional – and to some extent proprietorial – interest in the estate. At the time she was staying in a house called 'Weston' in St. Marychurch owned by a pair of sisters called Patteson. (They were the sisters of John Coleridge Patteson who was Bishop of Melanesia from 1861 until his murder by natives in 1871.)

'Weston' appears to have been run as a high-class boarding establishment, and Mary Brunel stayed there on several occasions. This time a stay originally intended to last a few weeks was extended to a stay of months. Henry Brunel, writing to his brother Isambard with youthful cynicism, attributed the change of plan to a form of 'nosey-parkerism'. 'She is coming here for five months, having changed plans and decided to go to St. Marychurch so that she can make friends with Colonel Wright and bother him with advice upon the grounds.'

Watcombe Park 1903   © Devon Record Office

CHAPTER 10:
The Grounds Mature

A Walk around the Park in 1882

Whether Mary Brunel gave plentiful advice about the grounds – and whether Colonel Wright heeded it – has not been discovered. Colonel Wright's main enthusiasm, it appears, was for horses: he enjoyed being driven around the area in a carriage drawn by a fine team. He must, however, have used some of his wealth to ensure that the grounds were well-kept, for during his occupation there were two detailed reports on 'Watcombe Park' in the *Gardeners' Chronicle*. The first of these was in July 1882, and is of special interest for its description of how Brunel's planting had matured about thirty years after it was begun. (It is a fascinating thought that, had he lived to his father's age, Brunel, aged seventy-six, would have been alive to conduct the reporter around the estate.)

By this time Brunel's spectacular approach drive from Great Hill had been

Lodge & Ichabod Wright's fine Entrance Gates in 1903   © *National Monumental Record*

View Below Slopes 1903 - on the right, the rustic seat set into the bank   © *National Monumental Record*

abandoned, and the reporter approached from the Teignmouth Road through 'massive gates set in ornamental stone columns, which are of the most substantial and expensive character.' (There must have been standing instructions to flatter the proprietor, resulting in this ripe specimen of journalese.) There were fine trees and shrubs along the drive leading to the mansion – 'a noble building…set among plants and shrubs of the choicest and most valuable description.'- (yet more flattery.) There was praise for the view from the terrace, and then the reporter – a plantsman it appears – began a detailed description of flower-beds and shrubberies. Here is Brunel's Watcombe Garden Book come to life, the fruition of all his scheming. The Italian Garden was already well-sheltered by the planned hedges of yew with a background of Monterey Cypress: but 'the greatest feast is in store for the visitor who has time to explore the "lower pleasure grounds" and who knows something of trees and plants.' A pond is described, a rustic seat set into a bank [both features that have survived], and then comes a tribute to the skill of the valley planting. 'The irregular curves of the banks and shrubbery beds in front of them indicate the care and skill that was taken in laying out these grounds by the great Brunel, who, with a man named Forsyth, carried out the work, except what trifling alterations have since been made upon the original plan.' Here is interesting

The Horse Shoe Slope 1903. Brunel's trees now fifty years old. © *National Monumental Record*

confirmation that Brunel was responsible for the main features of the planting – not Vicary or Crompton or Wright.

Already in existence in Brunel's time, and appearing on the 1859 estate map, was a horseshoe-shaped bed sited in a south-facing and sheltered position to contain the tenderest plants. After listing these the visitor moved on to the foot of the valley, where 'Brunel's Rockery and Water-Garden' was much admired: (the fact that it was given this title from early days is an indication that Brunel probably worked on its design and construction himself – presumably in the seedy dress noted by Arthur James.) The planting here was described in detail and much admired: 'one pond had an

island in its centre with a plant of *Osmunda regalis* looking really royal and at home in its quarters which could not have been better selected.' Climbing out of the valley by the Horse-shoe Steps, the reporter returned by a fern-bordered walk, to visit the range of hot-houses, most of which had probably been inherited from Mr. Forsyth. The tour ended with a quick glance at the fruit and kitchen gardens: 'in them may be seen the usual stock of fruit and vegetables.' With this dismissive remark, the reporter probably went off to take tea with the head gardener, Mr. Sandford, who like the reporter must have been both plantsman and North-countryman. 'Although he has for the time being retired from the din and battle of horticultural contests, his zeal as a cultivator has in no way diminished, nor has his enthusiasm waxed cold, since his removal from those stirring scenes which are less frequent in the West of England than in the busy go-ahead Northern Counties.' (The two of them must have had a lively time discussing the slow pace of folk in Devon, reckoned by some detractors to have only two speeds – dead-slow and stop.)

A longer Walk around the Park in 1887

Watcombe's reputation must have spread around, because only five years later, in October 1887, a second report appeared in the *Gardeners' Chronicle*. 'Many who have seen the grounds pronounce them the most beautiful to be met with in this delightful part of the West, and it would indeed be difficult to point to a more lovely spot.' This time there was no mention of Mr. Sandford, head gardener: perhaps he had returned to his 'go-ahead' Northern counties. Tribute was paid instead to Alexander Forsyth 'who a short time back [two years earlier] was called away from the field in which his long labours had been spent, alike with credit to himself and to the pursuit of which he was a worthy and respected member…Mr. Forsyth was entrusted by Mr. Brunel with the laying out of the grounds. How well he acquitted himself in the work is shown by the appearance of the place at the present day, when some thirty years have elapsed since the planting was

completed, and which, though long enough to allow a good portion of the sands of human life to run out, is a long way short of being sufficient for the full development of trees.'

The earlier reporter had been a plantsman: here we have a man of the trees. He pays brief attention to the borders near the house 'filled with a number of the finest kinds of exotic shrubs, deciduous and evergreen.' But quickly he is carried away by the Cupressus Macrocarpa – 'magnificent trees in the most perfect condition from base to top - not one of them showing the falling-off which this tree often exhibits in many places after it has been planted for some time. The different varieties of Retinospora [Japanese Cypress] thrive in a way calculated to make those who live in less favoured places regret that these beautiful evergreen trees will not succeed everywhere.' Both of the steep slopes rising from the valley were 'well planted with deciduous and evergreen trees, including the best and most distinct of each section, which collectively have attained a size, in the little over thirty years they have been planted, that could scarcely be credited.' (Reposing in some well-engineered Valhalla, Brunel must have been gratified to find his labours so fully appreciated!) Special praise was given to a Japanese Red Cedar and to a Monterey Cypress, both with branches feathered perfectly down to the ground.

A walk along the western side of the valley provided an opportunity to enjoy

'Standing on the walk about midway from the mansion to the opposite end of the valley, with one's back to the evening sun, the opposite slope presented as effective an example of leaf-colouring as could well be imagined: the variety of hues, from the black-green of the Austrian Pine to the pale tints of the Deodars, in contrast with the purple Beeches and the light and the dark leaves of other deciduous trees, was a good illustration of what may be done in this direction when the planter knows what he is about.'
© Brunel Manor

the effects of evening sunshine upon the foliage on the opposite hillside. Here comes the tribute to Brunel's craftsmanship, part of which was quoted earlier. 'Standing on the walk about midway from the mansion to the opposite end of the valley, with one's back to the evening sun, the opposite slope presented as effective an example of leaf-colouring as could well be imagined: the variety of hues, from the black-green of the Austrian Pine to the pale tints of the Deodars, in contrast with the purple Beeches and the light and the dark leaves of other deciduous trees, was a good illustration of what may be done in this direction when the planter knows what he is about.' Brunel's artistry was also perceived by the fashion in which the visitor was exposed to 'the unexpected' – an important quality in landscape design. 'Another of these long shady walks leads to the open ground at the bottom end of the park, where a good view of the

mansion with its beautiful grounds is obtained. In fact, one of the features of Watcombe is that at every turn something unexpected presents itself to the eye.'

Fortunately this reporter had the time, enthusiasm and stamina to carry on where his colleague had broken off for his tea and chat. He went on to explore the Sea Walk and enjoy the experience which Brunel and Forsyth had so carefully prepared. Crossing the road by 'a rustic foot-bridge' – the one designed by Brunel and erected by his son Henry – he was soon enjoying 'one of the most beautiful views which the kingdom affords.' Across Lyme Bay the coastal towns were bathed in autumn sunshine. Closer at hand were '…numerous small craft and pleasure-boats, the sails of which hung limp and unmoved by the lazy wind that was too listless to move a ripple on the glassy surface of the sea.'

The Vista - Brunel's Green Lane in its heyday. In the distance, the sea in the bay appeared to be a lake - a feature admired by Brunel. © Brunel Manor

View from south east showing Brunel's conifers along the sea walk c1870 © Devon Record Office

Walking further along the grassy ride he admired the varieties of conifer giving both shade and shelter: '...they thrive amazingly, unaffected by the sea breeze or the winds from the land side, to which they are equally exposed.' Brunel's selection of trees for this windy site was recognized by a man who could appreciate his skill.

Next he moved on to the section of the Sea Walk above Giant Rock, 'where the high ground terminates abruptly with a rocky perpendicular descent to the sea, which is so far below as to make one feel safer when at a respectful distance from the edge. Here the English Channel is in full view.' Having imposed this frisson on the visitor, the Sea Walk then doubled back parallel to the Teignmouth road. Here again the trees were '...fully exposed to the fierce western gales, but which do not perceptibly affect them.' A minor note of criticism finally appears.

'Here, as in the majority of places, the result of not thinning out sufficiently before the trees get too much crowded shows itself in the injured branches of many that should have been treated so as to admit of their retaining their lower branches down to the ground.' (Possibly they had not received due attention from the new owners: but since a main objective was to provide a windbreak the close planting was perhaps deliberate.) A tour of the glasshouses produced the information that the family were in residence only during the winter. The amount of fruit grown under glass was therefore very limited, but all the usual greenhouse plants 'were in a highly creditable condition.' If Mr. Sandford had moved on his successor was doing the place proud; the vegetables were 'well done, and the general keeping of the place is such as to show the skilful management brought to bear upon it.'

CHAPTER 11:
Brunel's Heritage at Watcombe

'The Glory has departed'

The name Ichabod had been handed down in the Wright family from around 1700. For nearly two centuries the family flourished as bankers and landowners in the Nottingham area, and much of modern Nottingham has been built upon their land. When Colonel Wright came to Watcombe in 1876 it must have been with hopes of establishing his family in Devon – at least as winter residents. Three years later, in 1879, the first tragedy struck. The Colonel's eldest son, Lt. Ichabod Denman Wright, arrived in India as an artillery officer during the Second Afghan War. 'Cheerful and zealous', he sought the first opportunity to go forward with reinforcements. Near the frontier fort of Jagdalak the column was ambushed and Lt. Wright was fatally wounded. He was buried that evening below the ramparts of the fort, far from the Watcombe Park that he must have hoped one day to inherit.

Other troubles followed, and by the time Colonel Wright died in 1901 the family was beset with financial difficulties and lawsuits. By 1903 the oldest family estate of Mapperley was sold by auction – by Chancery Court order - to meet debts owed to the Capital and County Bank:

other legal battles dragged on between 1902 and 1907 which brought the family to its knees. More and more land was mortgaged and later sold. That family name of Ichabod, 'the glory has departed', is deeply symbolic of the subsequent fate of Brunel's landscaping masterpiece at Watcombe. How has this been allowed to happen? Partly, of course, this results from our habit of type-casting our heroes. Brunel was renowned as an engineer – so all his engineering works must be cherished and treated with respect: except among a few, he had no reputation as landscaper, and his achievement could be disregarded and allowed to wither away.

The Watcombe Estate dismantled

At one time the bulk of the Watcombe estate was offered to Torquay Council – but the local Councils were already absorbing more property than even a boa-constrictor could digest. In Torquay the great estates of 'Torre Abbey' and 'Cockington' were purchased in the Thirties: in Paignton there was 'Oldway Mansion', developed by the sewing-machine profits of the Singer family. (If only it had proved possible for a far-sighted Council to have purchased 'Watcombe', later permitting some

Aerial view showing the estate in the mid 1900's. The walled kitchen garden had become a nursery and contained extensive greenhouses   © Brunel Manor

limited housing development with due regard to the landscape!) Gradually running downhill, the nucleus of the estate passed from the Wrights to Sir John Edwards Moss; then in 1923 to Frederick James Lund, and finally in 1932 to Thomas John Crossman, a local timber merchant. Most of the original estate has been sold off in small parcels; the usual criterion being, not how the buildings might be best related to Brunel's landscape, but how the maximum number might be inserted

through skilful distribution. One bright spot is that the mansion itself, renamed 'Brunel Manor', together with some twelve acres of surrounding grounds, was purchased by the Holiday Fellowship and opened as a Christian Holiday Home. (In 1963 house and land passed to the present owners, the Woodlands House of Prayer, and their occupation has been handled with sensitivity and respect. Above all the site has been left largely intact, and exciting finds are now being made, linking the present layout to

Brunel's Watcombe Garden Book where he set out his plans in the 1850's).

Brunel's park and arboretum were at one time threatened by a proposal to run a road up the central valley and open it up to housing. This was vetoed, and a complex pattern of land exchanges took place in 1966. The Council released land to allow access for development on other parts of the estate, while securing the main parkland, (now known as Brunel Woods), as Public Open Space. Early in 1987 a Brunel in Devon Trust was formed to help preserve not just the arboretum but also Brunel's more extensive heritage in South Devon:

'The signature of Brunel is truly written across this piece of countryside,' people were told, 'though it takes some finding!' Later that year Watcombe was registered as a Historic Park, and in 1988 Torbay council designated an extensive Watcombe Park Conservation

Lady Campbell, Brunel's Great great granddaughter, assisting with the tree replanting in Brunel Woods following the storm damage in 1990
© Herald Express, Torquay

Keith Barratt carving Brunel's Wellingtonia into the memorial column
Image Peter Lemar

Area. Such registration and designation provided no defence against the destruction that so swiftly followed. On 25th January, 1990, winds of up to 100 mph felled many of Brunel's trees, though fortunately the valley sheltered most of the finest specimens. In October that year Task Force Trees made a grant for clearing and replanting – a task which engaged the interest and support of many local people. A fallen Wellingtonia was shaped into an elegant column, and on 8th December 1992 this was erected at the lower end of Brunel's Green Lane. This input of central funding for remedial work was all to the good, but a historic site of this quality needs continuing skilled oversight and adequate maintenance funds. As argued in the Afterword, Brunel's woodlands should perhaps be viewed as a national memorial and receive proper national funding.

The case for preserving Brunel's landscaping masterpiece

'...Unprotected, deserted and abandoned!' Brunel used these words in 1846, when he saw his splendid *Great Britain* lying 'like a useless saucepan' on an exposed Irish shore. One hundred and sixty years later they come close to describing the present condition of Brunel's great landscape. Through Brunel's persistence *Great Britain* was salvaged the following year; and the ship was finally brought back from the Falkland Islands to Bristol in 1970. Could a determined salvage operation be performed now, to save the remnants of Brunel's Watcombe Park? At first sight the past century's ravages may appear so damaging, that not much can remain worth saving: fortunately that is far from correct. In September 1987 the Brunel in Devon Trust produced an 'Outline Plan for I.K. Brunel's Heritage Park at Watcombe, Devon.' The proposals won considerable interest, but Torquay had plenty on its plate elsewhere, and Brunel was not yet the cult figure – voted second in the 'Great Britons' Contest – which he has since become. Elements of the proposed Heritage Park, such as Portland Villa and Mrs Peek's Teafield, have since disappeared: but much remains to marvel at. A visiting Frenchman paused for a moment when walking along one of Brunel's cobble-lined rides. He spread his arms expansively – in the way that Frenchmen have. 'Mais c'est une vraie cathédrale d'arbres!' he declared. 'Why, this is a veritable cathedral of trees!'

But not of trees alone. There is still plenty to enjoy, for those who have eyes to see and an imagination to use. Moor Lane and Steps Lane were laid out by Brunel and are lined with the massive

The fallen Wellingtonia shaped into an elegant column, was erected at the lower end of Brunel's Green Lane on 8th December 1992 as a memorial to Brunel's achievements. Image Tracey Elliot-Reep

The remains of Brunel's Rockery At the foot of the valley
Image Tracey Elliot-Reep

banks his navvies built and by the beech trees he planted. (Several wells survive – one has been preserved as an important feature in a bungalow garden.) At the top of Steps Lane is the stretch of wall Brunel laid out when 'down on Saturday;' and just beyond is the flight of steps, inserted to placate that St. Marychurch Vestry. At the foot of the valley lie the remains of Brunel's Rockery and Water Garden, which he planned so carefully and where he must have laboured so hard; and nearby is the column carved by Keith Barrett, portraying aspects of Brunel's engineering - and the wooden figure of

the man himself taking pleasure in his parkland, 'Brunel's Dance'. The Woodland Walks present the extensive views across Torbay that drew Brunel to Watcombe, and then come the Monkey Puzzle trees to which he gave such devoted attention. The Monterey Cypresses are now so huge that most folk suggest they must be around 500 years old – yet this tree only reached this country in 1838.

Below 'Brunel Manor' is the steep slope which the ladies in the British Association party in 1869 attempted so uproariously – and so unsuccessfully –

to climb. Nearby is Brunel's upper water-garden, now being explored: (sections of water-pipe have been found, laid no doubt by Simpson's water-engineers, just as scheduled by Brunel in his Watcombe Garden Book.) In front of the Manor lie those borders where Arthur James encountered Brunel 'in seedy dress' at Easter 1858 – busy with his wife laying out the gardens. Further on lie the stables, where Colonel Wright indulged himself with his fine horses; and the gardener's cottage where Forsyth drank his holly-leaf tea and Mr. Sandford discussed the superior merits of Northcountrymen. The walled kitchen garden still exists – though with a crop of bungalows now instead of winter vegetables: and along the ridge runs the shelter-belt of beeches. (This is where Brunel grudgingly agreed to pay Mr. Blackaller up to £200 as a final offer for two acres of indifferent land.) The avenue of trees stretching along the flanks of Great Hill was felled in the 1980's – but could perhaps be replanted, being such an important element in Brunel's designed landscape: and so we come to Great Hill, extracted from the Admiralty by Brunel with so much care. From here one can appreciate the full extent of Brunel's achievement. During his short time at Watcombe he did more than fashion a garden and a park: with his tree-planting he created a landscape. His trees, now 150 years old and of great size, still sweep up the slopes and march along the ridges to dominate the eastern skyline of Torbay.

The Monterey Cypresses are now so huge that most folk suggest they must be around 500 years old. Image Tracey Elliot-Reep

Brunel's upper water-garden, now being explored: (sections of water-pipe have been found, laid no doubt by Simpson's water-engineers, just as scheduled by Brunel in his Watcombe Garden Book.)
Image Tracey Elliot-Reep

In front of the Manor lie those borders where Arthur James encountered Brunel 'in seedy dress' at Easter 1858
Image Tracey Elliot-Reep

The kitchen garden wall still exists   Image Tracey Elliot-Reep

Along the ridge runs the shelter-belt of beeches. (This is where Brunel grudgingly agreed to pay Mr. Blackaller up to £200 as a final offer.)   Image Tracey Elliot-Reep

The elegant balustrade was added to Brunel's original ha ha by Col Ichabod Wright   Image Tracey Elliot-Reep

Yew Trees discovered in the Italian Garden during restoration in 2006   Image Helen Hillard

The Terrace Pond & Fountain   Image Tracey Elliot-Reep

Andy Maltas restoring Italian Garden   Image Helen Hillard

Brunel's semi circular seat area was uncovered in 2006 when restoration commenced   *Image Tracey Elliot-Reep*

Semi circular seat before restoration began. See this area in its original glory on p125.   *Image Helen Hillard*

Approach to the Great Bridge over the Teignmouth Road   Image Helen Hillard

The original bridge over the Teignmouth Road   Image Helen Hillard © Devon Record Office

BRUNEL'S ARBORETUM

Brunel's Trees at Watcombe

(From an article in the Torquay Directory, 23 Sept. 1871 by a correspondent signing himself G)

A BIT OF SOUTH DEVON
[From the Journal of Horticulture]

Passing over a few miles of Devon lanes, skirted by cider orchards, a ruin of a very different kind is to be visited. It is at Watcombe, the ruin of a residence never erected. This is no paradox. About twenty and two years since, Brunel the younger saw here a coombe, from the high grounds around which most extensive views inland and seaward are commanded. He purchased that coombe and its surroundings, wisely commenced planting forthwith, that the trees might be growing while the house was erecting. In the valley he plotted out the flower garden; on the hills around he planted his arboretum; he built a gardener's house; he formed an Italian garden, and adjoining it laid the foundation of a residence. It is said that foundation cost him three thousand pounds and then he proceeded no further. Why he stayed proceedings your penman knoweth not, but he does know that someone needing a mansion and grounds suitable to his wealth should become the purchaser, and complete the work. When Mr. Brunel died, the estate was purchased by two brothers named Vickery, residing at Newton Abbot; but they only purchased to sell it again for a fairer price.

The gardens and plantations are kept in excellent order by Mr. Helstone, the intelligent and obliging gardener, and those plantations are worth a journey to wander among. The whole estate includes sixty acres, and of these the pinetum occupies twenty acres and the Crataeguses nearly two acres. The Coniferae are perfect specimens, so vigorous, so clothed with branches to the very soil's surface, and so well apart that on every side they are symmetrical. Mr. Helstone obligingly furnished me with a list of the three chief collections of trees. Those of the Coniferae to which an asterix (*) is prefixed are all well furnished with cones this year, and he thinks several with perfect seeds for the first time. He has raised thousands of seedlings, from seeds ripened here, of Cupresus macrocarpa and Pinus insignis.

CONIFERS ON WATCOMBE ESTATE AND HEIGHTS

Abies alba, 20 feet high
    glauca
      *Douglassaii, 50 feet
      taxifolia, 20 feet
      excelsa, 50 feet
          Clanbrasiliana, 2 feet
          Stricta
          Elegans
    Gregorrii
    *Menziesii, 35 feet
    Morinda
    *nigra, 20 feet
    orientalis
*Araucaria imbricata, 35 feet
      Biota orientalis
      aurea, 3 feet
      compacta
      glauca
      incurvata
    meldensis, 10 feet
    tartarica
Cedrus argentea variegata, 20 ft
    Deodara, 40 feet
      viridis, 20 feet
    Libani, 30 feet
Cephalotaxus drupacea, 10 feet
    Fortunii
    Harringtonii
Cryptomeria japonica, 35 feet
    Lobbii, 20 feet
    nana, 5 feet
Cupressus Corneyana
    elegans, 20 feet
    Goveniana
    Lambertiana
    Uhdeana
    torulosa
    lusitanica, 10 feet
    Lawsoniana
    macrocarpa, 50 feet
Juniperus chinensis, 12 feet
    hibernica
    excelsa
    recurva, 12 feet
    thurifera
    spherica
    Sabina, 2 feet

Libocedrus Doniana, 3 feet
    Chilensis, 10 feet
Picea argentea, 20 feet
    bracteata
    *cephalonica, 35 feet
    Fraserei
    Lasoicarpa, 10 feet
    *nobilis, 25 feet
    *Nordmanniana
    Pinsapo
    *Webbiana
Pinus austriaca, 30 feet
    Laricio
    Mugho, 15 feet
    uliginosa
    muricata
    Pinea (Stone Pine) 20 feet
    pumilio, 10 feet
    Benthamiana, 30 feet
    insignis, 35 feet
    Gerardiana, 20 feet
    Jeffreyi
    ponderosa
    Sabiniana
    tubercaulata
    ayacahuite
    Cembra
    excelsa
    Hartweggii
    Lambertiana
    Monterzumae
    monticola
    Strobus
Retinospora ericoides
Taxus adpressa
    baccata
      canadensis
      fastigiata
      Dovastoni
    elegantissima
Thuja gigantea, 10 feet
    Lobbii
    variegata
Thujopsis borealis, 20 feet
    dolabrata, 5 feet
Wellingtonia gigantea, 30feet

OAKS

Quercus pendula
    agrifolia
    castanelfolia
    Cerris
    heterophylla
    Lucumbeana
    variegata argentea
    cocifera
    coccinea
    densiflora
    faginea
    glabra
    Fordii
    dentata
    larifolia
    rotundifolia
    salicifolia

Quercus Mirbeckii
    Ilex serratifolia
    palustris
    pedunculata
        asplenifolia
        Purpurea
    nigra
    pterifolia
    pyramidalis
    maculata
    marginata
    rubra
    Suber
    Turneri
    imbricata
    taraxacifolia
    sideroxla
    virens

HAWTHORNS

Cratægus apiifolia
    Aronia
    coccinea
    crenulata
    Crus-galli
    Douglasii
    flava
    glandulosa
    heterophylla
    intermedia
    latifolia
    lobata
    lucida
    Macnabiana
    macrantha
    Oxyacantha
        melanocarpa
        fructu-coccineo
    Celsina

Cratægus neapolitana
    nigra
    odoratissima
    orientalis
    ovalifolia
    mexicana
    coccinea
    Guthrieana
    laciniata pendula
    pendula ala
    plena alba
    stricta
    prunifolia
    purpurea
    pryifolia
    glabra
    tomentosa
    trilobata
    virginiana

BEECHES

Fagus betuloides
    asplenifelia, or salicifolia

Fagus sylvatica pendula
    purpurea

Castanea Sativa (Spanish Chestnut Or Sweet Chestnut)
Image Tracey Elliot-Reep

Picea Sitchensis (Sitka Spruce)
Image Tracey Elliot-Reep

Thujopsis Dolabrata (Hiba)
Image Tracey Elliot-Reep

Juniperus Chinensis (Chinese Spruce)
Image Tracey Elliot-Reep

Brunel's Watcombe Estate – the continuing story

1847 — Brunel bought the first plot of land for his Watcombe Estate. Appointed Alexander Forsyth as gardener and began landscaping his estate with expert advice from William Nesfield, a leading garden designer at that time.

1851 — Brunel commissioned William Burn, an exclusive country house architect, to draw up plans for the house.

1859 — Brunel had an estate map drawn up as he realised it would have to be sold when he died. This shows the extent of the woodlands he planted, water arrangements, kitchen gardens, track ways, terraces, the Italian garden and the outline of the house, only the cellars of which had been completed. The whole estate was 100 acres plus a quarter share in 36 acres of common land at this time.

1863 — The estate was bought by John and Robert Vicary. William Elston, employed by Brunel in 1856 to succeed Alexander Forsyth as head gardener, continued to manage the grounds.

1870 — Mr James Roper Crompton purchased Watcombe. He was a wealthy paper manufacturer who owned extensive mills near Bury in Lancashire. He built the existing house to a modified design, using the floor plan of the foundations and cellars left by Brunel. He also built the stables, extended the gardener's lodge and built new workers cottages at Peasland. It was Crompton who named the estate Watcombe Park. He died in 1874 and the estate was for sale again with a schedule of work still to be completed estimated at £2,092.

1876 — Watcombe Park was bought for £22,900 by Col Ichabod Wright of Staplefore Hill, Nottingham. He built the ballroom/tennis court and the magnificent adjoining domed conservatory & palm house and added the elegant arched entrance to the stable block. He also erected the elaborate entrance gates and had the balluststrades constructed round the terrace on top of Brunel's existing ha ha wall. He went into bankruptcy and in 1903, arrangements were made for the estate to be sold off. Ichabod Wright died in May 1905, but the legal battles continued within the family until the estate was finally sold.

1907 — The estate was sold for £15,000 to Sir Thomas John Edwards Moss, second baronet and eldest son of the first baronet of Otterspool at Roby. The name of Watcombe Park was changed to Roby Hall.

1923 — The estate sold for £17,500 to Fredrick James Lund. He reinstated the name Watcombe Park. Large portions of land were disposed of to Torbay Council.

1931 — Watcombe Park was sold to Thomas John Crossman of Ashe, Churston Ferrers, Devon. By now the estate had reduced to 65 acres, the workers cottages at Peasland and the same 1/4 share in the Watcombe Common land that Brunel had secured.

1932 — The house and approximately twelve acres of land was sold to The Holiday Fellowship who made it a Christian holiday home. During the Second World War (1940 – 1945) Stockwell Teacher Training College evacuated here from Bromley and the Stable block became a billet for soldiers. The Lodge continued as a guest house. The Holiday Fellowship renamed the mansion Brunel Manor.

1963 — The Woodlands House Of Prayer Trust purchased Brunel Manor to use it as a Christian Holiday and Conference Centre. The trust has also bought the lodge and the stable block. In 2006, as part of the Brunel 200 Celebrations, restoration of Brunel's original features in the grounds at the Manor began. The gardens are now open to the public on a regular basis.

Much of the land originally owned by Brunel has been developed with housing. However large areas of his woodlands remain. The Brunel Woods, owned by Torbay Council, are open to the public at all times and are managed by the Torbay Coast and Countryside Trust.

AFTERWORD

Brunel created his landscape, not for himself alone, but for his own generation and future generations to enjoy. Undervalued for years, there is now a growing awareness that this site should be regarded as a national treasure.

In January 2004 Torbay Heritage Forum produced its Vision of the Future:

- Our heritage is important

- An impressive legacy

- Deserves a high level of care

In discussing Torbay's Key Heritage Assets the Forum agreed that 'highest priority is given to assets that are of national heritage significance, are at risk, and provide public access, learning or employment opportunities.' (Brunel's landscape scores heavily under all these headings.) The main difficulties were also listed:

- Lack of funding for capital projects to restore and realise the potential of our heritage assets

- Lack of funding for basic maintenance

- Difficulties in conserving landscape-scale features in multiple ownership

Some recent funding has made possible a start on garden and woodland restoration: perhaps Brunel's landscape may at last be recognised as a national treasure, and win the resources required for its regeneration.

BIBLIOGRAPHY

Manuscripts and other Primary Sources

1: In the University of Bristol Library: Special Collections

Private Letter Books: (letters about Watcombe appear among general engineering business.
The number is much reduced after 1849 when Brunel had his house down at Watcombe.)

Large Sketch Books: (Most of the material dealing with Watcombe is in vol 2)

Small Sketch Books: (Some additional material, mostly quick sketches)

Watcombe Garden Book: (Brunel's garden notes and memoranda, 1849-1858. This recently rediscovered notebook is evidence of Brunel's 'hands-on' approach.)

Watcombe Photograph: (A view of the gardens at Watcombe, probably 1860-64)

Henry Marc Brunel Letterbooks: (Henry used the newly perfected letterpress to produce duplicates of all his outgoing mail. These provide important information on events after Brunel's death – for example the chapel at the Barton estate.)

2: Devon County Record Office, Exeter:

Tithe Maps and Apportionments: (These show how the land at Watcombe was divided at the time into small fields held by many landowners.)

St.Marychurch – Stokeinteignhead Road Closure Documents, 1848: (These demonstrate in great detail how much had to be done to close a public road.)

Watcombe Park Estate map, 1859: (This is the map completed by Dawson, Brunel's Surveyor, and carefully checked by Brunel when close to death.)

Watcombe Park Sale Details, 27.7.1876

G.D.C. Tudor Archive – Deposit No. 6091: (Collection of research material including photocopies, drawings, photographs and slides. For example, it includes the Dubois Survey of Watcombe Park in 1990 after the Great Storm.)

3: Torquay Reference Library:
Torquay Directory and other
local sources

4: The Royal Archives, Windsor
Material relating to the 1851
Exhibition and artisan housing

5: James, Arthur: (Documents held
by his descendants)
Memoirs (unpublished)

Printed Works

Acland, Anne: A Devon Family,
the Story of the Aclands, 1981

Brindle, Steven: Brunel, 2005

Brunel in Devon Trust: Outline Plam
for I.K. Brunel's Heritage Park, 1987

Brunel, Isambard: The Life of Isambard
Kingdom Brunel, Civil Engineer, 1870

Buchanan, R.A.: Brunel, 2002

Carter, Tom: The Victorian Garden,
1984

Cherry Bridget and Pevsner Nikolaus:
The Buildings of England, Devon, 1989

Corlett, E.W.: The Iron Ship, 1975

Fisher, Michael: Alton Towers, a Gothic
Wonderland, 1999

Horsley, John Calcott: Recollections of
a Royal Academician, 1903

Noble, Celia: The Brunels, Father and
Son, 1938

Pateman, L. Ed.: Pictorial and
Historical Survey of Babbacombe &
St. Marychurch Vol 2, 1991

Pugsley, Sir Alfred Ed: The Works of
Isambard Kingdom Brunel, 1976

Rolt, L.T.C.: Isambard Kingdom
Brunel, 1957

Russell, Percy: Torquay, 1960

Shephard, Sue; Seeds of Fortune,
A Gardening Dynasty, 2003 [Veitch
Family]

Thomas, Graham Stuart: Gardens of
the National Trust, 1979

Thomas, Graham Stuart: Trees in the
Landscape, 1983

Thomas, Graham Stuart Ed:
Recreating the Period Garden, 1984

Tudor, Geoffrey: The Brunels in
Torbay, 1989

Vaughan, Adrian: Isambard Kingdom
Brunel, Engineering Knight-Errant,
1991

Wilson, Richard and Mackley, Alan:
Creating Paradise: The Building of the
English Country House 1660-1880

ACKNOWLEDGEMENTS

The production of this book has been the result of much co operation by a number of people:

- Bristol University Archives for much help with research and supply of images

- Devon records for assistance with research and availability of images

- Torquay Library for help with some of the research.

- Torquay Museum staff who have helped with research, availability of images and who worked along side us for the Brunel 200 Celebrations of 2006.

- Peter and Joan Lemar, for background information, photographs, encouragement and support for the project.

- The current generation of Brunel's descendents who have encouraged the production of this book and given valued help, general background information and advice.

- The Brunel Manor staff and volunteers who have contributed in many ways and who made the success of the opening of the Gardens for the Brunel 200 celebrations a reality.

INDEX

Admiralty	85-88, 117, 137
Alton Towers	24, 65
Atmospheric railway	12, 19, 26
Barn Close - cottages, school/chapel	12, 72-76
Bennett - Brunel's secretary	25, 33-34, 112
British Association	121, 136
Brunel, Florence	59, 102, 109
Brunel, great great grandchildren	6, 133
Brunel, Henry	6-7, 46, 76, 105, 108, 116-117, 119-123, 128
Brunel, Isambard IKB's first son	7, 18, 29, 102, 103, 117, 123
Brunel, Isambard Kingdom	5, 12, 13, 30, 42, 50, 76, 93, 101, 111, 117, 121, 135, 151
Brunel, Mary	10, 12, 15, 35, 39, 58, 81, 84, 104, 110, 121, 123, 124
Brunel, Sir Marc Isambard	13, 38, 49, 104, 105
Brunel Manor	5-6, 8, 132, 136, 137, 151
Brunel - memorial column	134-135
Brunel's letters	24-26, 48, 49, 73, 85, 100-101, 108-109, 118, 120
Burn, William - Architect	12, 87, 90-91, 148
Chelston Cross	102, 108, 116-118

Crompton, James Roper	122, 126
Crossman	132
Dawson, Brunel's cartographer	12, 24-26, 30-31, 38, 41, 48-49, 112
Driveway	36-37
Duke Street, London	12-13, 15, 19, 24-26, 33, 101, 103
Elston - gardener for Brunel	108, 121
En Avant - Brunel Family Motto	50-51
Fete Champetre	80
Forsyth, Alexander - Brunel's head gardener	10, 12, 17, 24, 26, 33, 41, 43-44, 49, 65-66, 69, 71, 104, 108, 125-128, 137
Froude, William	104-105, 108, 116, 117-118, 120
Grant, William Henry	31, 46, 49, 101
Great Bridge	119-120
Great Eastern	7, 10, 12, 25, 47-49, 85, 93, 101-103, 107, 110-111, 113
Great Exhibition, Crystal Palace	10, 12, 44, 54, 101
Great Hill	31, 35-37, 110, 124, 137
Hacqueville	17, 50, 105-106
Hesketh Crescent	22, 38
Horsley, John	15, 24, 51, 84, 93, 102
Italian Garden	63, 125, 144, 151
James, Arthur	12, 109, 112, 126, 137

Kitson	23, 25, 33-34, 41, 77
Langford-Brown Henry	25, 79
Map - Donn's 1765	18
Map - Estate 1859	114-115
Map - Parish	19
Map - Road closure	28
Mickleton Tunnel - Battle of	23, 77
Nesfield, William - Landscape gardener	59, 61, 69, 71, 151
Noble, Celia	109
Park Crescent	24
Peek, James	111
Pond	61-62, 66, 125, 126
Portland Villa (Maidencombe House)	42, 93, 110-112, 135
Prince Albert	73-74, 101
Queen Victoria	23, 76, 91
Renkioi Hospital	12
Rolt L.T.C	10, 50, 103, 105
Saltash Bridge	38, 48, 50, 58, 102
School at Barton (See also Barn Close)	12, 72
Semi circular seat	125, 142
Shrubs	62, 125, 127
Simpson, William - water engineer	12, 44, 137
St Mary's Church	82, 84

Station - Dawlish	12, 19
Station - Exeter	12
Station - Newton Abbot	18, 76
Station - Paddington	12, 44, 45
Station - Teignmouth	12, 18
Station - Torquay	12, 18, 76
Station - Torre	23, 80
Teignmouth Road	31, 119, 125, 130
Terrace	6, 8, 70, 87, 112, 125
Thames Tunnel	13, 50, 54
Thomas, Lady Vanessa	6, 73
Torquay Council	81, 131
Trackways	32
Trees - Brunel's drawings	52-53
Trees - Brunel's measurements	43, 104, 105, 107, 108, 120
Trees - buying	43
Trees - planting	6, 8, 10, 12, 24-25, 31, 36, 44, 46-48, 51, 58-59, 61-62, 66, 69, 71, 85, 87, 102
Veitch of Exeter	43
Views	76, 128, 136, 144
Vomero	22, 26, 38

Watcombe	5, 6, 7, 8, 10-12, 17, 19-20, 22, 24-29, 31, 34, 36-43, 46, 48-51, 54, 58, 66, 71-72, 75, 77-81, 85, 86-87, 91, 93, 100-116, 119-122, 124-125, 127-128, 131, 133, 135-137
Watcombe Garden Book	6, 12, 50, 125, 133, 137
Watcombe house plans	88-90, 93-99
Watcombe Park	8, 10, 11, 29, 36, 43, 71-72, 121-122, 124, 131, 133, 135, 151
Watcombe Villa	38-40, 81, 93, 111
Water arrangements	54, 151
Watson, Rev Alexander	77, 82-87, 11
Webbs Royal Hotel	29, 35
Woodlands House of Prayer Trust	5, 7, 151
Woodley, Daniel	38, 54, 100
Wright, Col Ichabod	122, 131, 151